Kriya Yoga Vichara
Integrated Techniques and Philosophy
of Ramana Maharshi
and Paramahansa Yogananda

Ryan Kurczak

Copyright © 2016 Ryan Kurczak

All rights reserved.

ISBN-10: 1519706936
ISBN-13: 978-1519706935

The scanning, uploading and distribution of this book via the Internet or any other means without permission of the author is illegal. Please purchase only authorized print and electronic editions and do not participate in or encourage the piracy of copyrighted materials. Your support of the author's rights is appreciated.

Before practicing any meditation, yoga or breathing exercises outlined in this text, consult with your healthcare provider to make sure you are fit for such practices. The techniques and methods described in this work are meant for educational purposes only. The philosophy described is for your enjoyment.

DEDICATION

This book is dedicated to Babaji, Lahiri Mahasaya, Swami Sri Yukteswar, Paramahansa Yogananda, Roy Eugene Davis, Ramana Maharshi, Richard Fish, Paula K., Sage Vasistha, Mountain, Swami Venkatesananda, Melissa, Corey Dowds, Lynda, Michael G., Kayla K., Michael J., Bill. K., Sage Patanjali, Alan Watts, Krishnamurti, Ernst Wilhelm, Miriam H., Joel Goldsmith, Gene C., Terry M., Kali, members of Unity of Kanawha Valley, April W., Krishna, Ashok Singh, Megan K., Sri Shani, Neal S., Prabha, Chris J., Russel W., Daniel P., Jim Norton, Kurt B., Rose Marie, all family, friends, enemies, supporters, detractors, teachers, students and to all the rest of those great souls, known and unknown, present, past and yet to come, that contributed a little of their life, wisdom, time, energy and inspiration to make this work possible. May it be a blessing to all who find it valuable!

CONTENTS

	Foreword	i
1	Work and Knowledge	1
2	Advanced Spirituality	15
3	Guru and Initiation	41
4	Kriya Meditation Techniques	52
5	Additional Considerations	77
6	Kriya Meditation Routines	100
7	The Four Gatekeepers of Liberation	126
8	Contemplative Practices	148
9	Objects of Contemplation	159
10	Yogic Sleep	214
11	The Inner Alchemy of Kriya Yoga Vichara	231

FOREWORD

The sudden wealth of books, media and upsurge of interest in Kriya Yoga and Vedanta has had both a positive and negative effect on the spirituality of humankind. Positively, we have seen more individuals taking an interest in techniques and traditions that will one day unify the world and allow its people to live in harmony with one another. Eventually, it will also allow us to realize our direct connection to the infinite abstract intelligence within, which most of us call Divinity. Negatively, we have seen profound philosophies and potent methods for internal enlightenment denigrated to idolatry in the form of mindless guru worship and watered down through excessive focus on mechanical application.

Uncommon are the books that reveal the magnitude of the task of the process we call enlightenment. Uncommon are the teachings that explain the subtle nature of the process, which requires both intelligently applied devotion, artistic practice of techniques and a lifestyle that supports the whole endeavor.

Within these pages is my humble attempt at filling this void. Much more could be said, and this book itself needs to be taken for what it is, limitations and all. These pages are an attempt to give a baseline understanding of the profound philosophy and practices of Kriya Yoga and Self-inquiry.

The practices and philosophies outlined need to be personally applied and contemplated until direct realization dawns. They also, most likely, need to be supplemented by working with a coach or mentor skilled in the approach to spiritual growth described herein. This book is not the final say in the matter. It is simply a record of the fundamental skills and philosophy required to awaken.

After completing the rough drafts, I had first considered titling this work, *The Most Unpopular Book on Kriya Yoga and Vichara*. Why you might ask? Because those souls for whom this book is written are rare, and those who may think they want to read this book probably will not like it. So let us clear up for whom this book is written and for whom it is not.

This book is not for people who need a churchlike communal experience and are averse to engaging the solitary path required for authentic inner transformation. It is not for those who feel that there is one-true-rocket-ship-technique that will magically elevate their consciousness to blissful realms. It is not for those looking for an escape from the world or for those seeking a relationship with a long dead savior-guru figure.

Now do you see why I thought of calling this work, *The Most Unpopular Book on Kriya Yoga and Vichara*? The majority who are typically drawn to the teachings of Ramana Maharshi and Paramahansa Yogananda most often fall into the ranks of those for whom this book is not written. However, over the many years in this field, I have seen that this is not always the case. As mentioned previously, there are those rare gems of people who long for something other than the sensationalized fantastic propaganda dished out in gigantic spoonfuls by our skillful spiritual marketers. They long for a solid, realistic, down-to-earth process of inner awakening that works.

KRIYA YOGA VICHARA

This book is written for those people who understand that any endeavor in life requires hard work, personal sacrifice, dedication and commitment. It is written for those who understand that the Herculean path of Self-realization requires a reasonable and logical approach supported, but not compulsively ruled by, emotional zeal. Essentially, this book is written for mature individuals who are ready to take responsibility and regain mastery of their states of consciousness. It is written for those who are ready to do what is necessary to realize that omniscient abstract intelligence is their very Self, while living their normal unassuming lives.

Some might wonder why I have chosen to merge Kriya Yoga and Vichara. They may think it best to keep each path pure and separate. However, as you will see, the works of both Paramahansa Yogananda and Ramana Maharshi weave flawlessly together. Where Yogananda's work ends, Ramana's begins. Although, in reality, there is no separation. Yogananda himself sought counsel from Ramana and spoke of the encounter in *Autobiography of a Yogi*. Many statements in the prime Kriya Yoga text, The *Yoga Sutras of Patanjali*, speak to the same methods as taught by Ramana Maharshi. Kriya Yoga lays the foundation for effective Self-inquiry. With a calm mind and balanced nervous system, one can very effectively contemplate one's own true nature, and accept with greater certainty the truth which is revealed in the process.

Kriya Yoga and Vichara serve as a powerful combination for inner realization. This will be made clear to you in the pages that follow, so long as you diligently attempt to understand and attentively practice what is shared. But, before you invest your time and resources into what is offered herein, be sure you are one of the few for whom this book is written.

Sincerely,
Ryan Kurczak
Winter Solstice 2015

Ramana Maharshi & Paramahansa Yogananda
At Arunachala near Tiruvannamalai

Chapter One

WORK AND KNOWLEDGE

The devotion and love of my spiritual life has been rightly shared between the practice of Kriya Yoga in the tradition of Paramahansa Yogananda and study of the teachings of Sri Ramana Maharshi. Kriya created the foundation for deeper exploration and direct experience of yogic principles. The methods of Vichara brought the realization of these principles vividly into my awareness. Ultimately, I have found that one cannot be practiced without the other for complete awakening to occur.

The marriage of these methods of Kriya and Ramana's teachings on Vichara (Self-inquiry) always brought to my mind the opening passage of that august text, *Vasistha's Yoga*. "Verily, birds are able to fly with their two wings: even so both work and knowledge together lead to the supreme goal of liberation. Not indeed work alone nor indeed knowledge alone can lead to liberation: but, both of them together form the means to liberation."

I have found that Kriya is the work that prepares the mind, body and consciousness to realize the supreme knowledge of our infinite nature as divine, timeless light. Vichara provides and awakens this knowledge of our Self beyond question and doubt. Together, Kriya and the knowledge of Vichara, as Vasistha states, enable the soul to fly free in spiritual liberation. It is my sincerest wish that you, too, will endeavor to attempt this sacred union.

It is for you, who may naturally see value in practicing both Kriya Yoga and Vichara, that I have written this book. It is for you, who remember Patanjali's aphorism, "Intensity in spiritual practice, learning and application of personal mantras and perfect aligning of attention with the Seer within is Kriya Yoga," that I write this book. In this sutra, we see that spiritual practice requires both intensity and direct alignment with the omniscient Seer within. It is Kriya that gives the focus and framework for intensity in practice. It is Vichara that immediately aligns our experience with the omniscient Seer within.

As you will see, the combination of Vichara and Kriya in one's meditation practice is as enjoyable and natural as combining butter and honey. In fact, through the practices described in this text you will learn how both approaches support the other. Kriya is a method that precisely tunes our "spiritual radio" and aligns our "spiritual antenna." Vichara is the practice that gives us direct communication with and realization of that omniscient Seer spoken of by Patanjali. You will find that Vichara practiced after Kriya brings profound realizations.

Before we dive too deeply into the practice, let's first consider what Kriya Yoga and Vichara are in their own right. Then let's determine why they work so well together, as they are really two sides of the same coin. Or, as Vasistha would say, "two wings of the same bird."

Kriya harmonizes the pranic life force within the body. It calms, develops and refines the nervous system, thereby giving a greater capacity to process and understand the consciousness around and within us. Our body and minds act like antenna, and the inner and outer world of our consciousness is the information it receives and projects. Through Kriya, our inner power to comprehend and interact with the world of information that defines all our experiences increases.

The universe, with all its mundane, solid, subtle and ethereal dimensions, is alive. It is responsive to itself. We are part of that seamless whole, even though our present feeling might make us believe otherwise. This means that the state of our nervous system, mind, thoughts and feelings both influence and are influenced by this greater being. That which we think about, wonder about, and the emotions we consistently entertain has an impact on this greater being. If our thoughts and questions are clear and strong and processed through a clear and strong antennae (our consciousness), the greater being can provide clear and strong experiences or insights in response.

Kriya Yoga has been made popular through the work of Paramahansa Yogananda. It is often associated with specific pranayama procedures. However, we remember that the second chapter in the *Yoga Sutras of Patanjali* is entitled Kriya Yoga. Yogananda's teacher, Swami Sri Yukteswar, specifically encouraged Yogananda to teach Kriya based on Patanjali's work. To this end, we can see that the full practice of Kriya Yoga requires implementation of all the eight limbs of yoga as described by Patanjali. For more information on this, please see my book *Kriya Yoga: Continuing the Lineage of Enlightenment*. Or, find any competent teacher or text that clarifies the eight limbs of yoga as taught by Patanjali.

Kriya does implement very specific pranayama and meditation procedures. In this work, I have shared them as I had learned them from my Kriya Yoga teacher and as he learned them from Paramahansa Yogananda. We will be exploring these techniques, but do not lose sight, as so many people do, of the much larger system of Kriya Yoga that Patanjali shared with us more than 2,000 years ago. By full application of

Patanjali's eight limbs of yoga, with corresponding practice of the specific Kriya pranayamas, only then will you be fully preparing your body, mind and consciousness for complete realization. Only then will you truly be practicing Kriya Yoga.

Vichara is Self-inquiry. Our modern culture became most acutely aware of the practice of Vichara through the life of Sri Ramana Maharshi. However, the practice itself is an ancient and timeless method utilized by yogis to gain direct knowledge and realization of the Self, the omniscient Seer of all. Typically, to practice Self-inquiry well requires previous mental training and discipline. My previous training, which led to the capacity to practice Self-inquiry, was in the form of Kriya Yoga. This approach will be described fully. However, keep in mind that any meditation path, which allows you to internalize your awareness and discipline your mind and emotions, is sufficient preparation for Vichara.

But, what is Vichara in practice? It is a focused method of wondering, exploring and contemplating the true nature of our Self. Through it we inquire, "Who am I?", "From where does this world arise?", "How does suffering end?", "What is the nature of this world of experience?". If we practice well, then the answers dawn in our consciousness. It does not happen upon us like a great voice booming from the void saying, "You are so and so." It is a feeling response, a direct insight into the truth of the matter. It cannot be explained in words. The knowledge is too vast for our limited human minds to hold. Nevertheless, when we identify with the reality of our greater being, we KNOW the truth, beyond any doubt. It is as clear as knowing the color of our skin or the color of the sky. No matter who tries to tell us the sky is red or our skin is silver, we KNOW the truth. No need to argue. We rest certain.

Vichara works because, as stated above, the universe, our greater being, is responsive to that which we want to know. Vichara is practiced well, when we are singular in the question. That means, when we practice and we wonder, "Who am I?" there are no other thoughts, distractions or questions arising. That is a clear signal, and that is all we want to know. It is for this reason that Kriya is so helpful in the process. It gives us a great capacity to rest with a clear consciousness and to focus on one thing at a time. If we focus on God, we will eventually experience God. If we can focus on Vichara, we will eventually experience realization of our line of inquiry. The time it takes for realization to dawn is dependent on our capacity to be one-pointed and devoted to one question at a time. Kriya Yoga is the method for developing this capacity.

Consider how a computer works. Have you ever tried to make a computer do too many processes at once? What happens? It crashes or freezes. Now imagine that you let that computer boot up fully. All of its operations are in order. Like a computer, when you are patient and focused with your yoga practice, the results dawn with more clarity. You initiate one procedure at a time. Each procedure executes quickly and easily. Knowledge and realization dawns flawlessly and seemingly effortlessly.

Your consciousness works in this manner. If you are attempting to practice Vichara, and you are weakly holding the question "Who am I?" in your awareness, while simultaneously wondering how you are going to deal with your co-workers tomorrow, what you are going to eat for dinner, if you have enough money in your retirement account, why is it so cold in this room, etc., the likelihood you will realize anything profound is dim. But, when your nervous system is refined and your capacity to hold your attention is in one place or on one line of inquiry with strength, peacefully, you will realize that to which you direct your attention.

This is explained in the Yoga Sutras of Patanjali. Patanjali states that, Samadhi (or cognitive absorption with that which you want to know) occurs after one has the capacity to internalize attention (Pratyahara – the fifth limb of yoga), to focus attention in one direction (Dharana – the sixth limb of yoga) and to effortlessly rest awareness on that focal point, alert and without strain (Dhyana – the seventh limb of yoga). Then we experience oneness with the object of contemplation as if devoid of our own sense of individuality. All we know and are is that which we are contemplating.

Consider the sutras of Patanjali for clarification:

II.53 *"Pratyhara (complete internalization of attention from external experience) leads to perfect mastery of the senses."*
III.1 *"Dharana (concentration) is the fixation of the field of being within a focal point."*
III.2 *"When a single thought directs the field of being to a chosen focal point, dhyana (meditation) occurs."*
III.3 *"The field of being reflects objects [focused on] alone, as if empty of its own essence, during Samadhi (oneness – cognitive absorption with the object of contemplation)."*

When we first begin our Kriya practice, it is the first four limbs of yoga on which we focus. These are the yamas, niyamas, asana and pranayama.

Yoga Sutras verse 29 of chapter 2: *"Yama, niyama, asana, pranayama, pratyahara, dharana, dhyana and samadhi are the eight limbs."*

The yamas and niyamas are the universal disciplines and behavioral restraints that harmonize our direction in life with that of peace and clarity. They serve as the foundation for all yoga practice and yogic living. Without them, our practice may tend to extremes, hurting ourself and others.

Asana is the practice of strengthening our body and mind with the intention to be able to sit still and comfortable for meditation and higher contemplation. If our bodies are not strong enough to keep us awake and upright during meditation, or if we cannot sit still long enough to experience the benefits of meditation, we will not proceed efficiently along our course in yogic contemplation.

Once we are established in yogic lifestyle principles and we have developed the strength of body and mind to sit still, we proceed to pranayama. These are methods of breath awareness and breath control. They cleanse, balance, refine and strengthen our nervous and energetic systems so that when we finally are ready to internalize our attention for pratyahara, there will be minimal distractions arising from the body or mind.

These first four limbs may take months or years to master. It depends on your innate talents and the skill sets with which you begin. It depends on how consistent and intelligently you practice. Also, please remember that talent is overrated. Those who start with great talent often do not master their skill. They ride on that talent and rarely endeavor to improve. Many of the world's greatest masters, in any art or science, had little innate talent, but worked and worked to perfect their art. They earned and embodied the title master because of this.

As you study this text and apply what you learn, take your time. Deeply contemplate the methods of Self-inquiry described. Give your full attention to the Kriya techniques as you practice them. Begin sculpting your life to reflect the eight limbs of yoga described by Patanjali. Most of all, do not practice meditation or live your life half-heartedly or without full concentration. In this way, you will rapidly realize the truth of your eternal nature. One day, you will instantly wake up to the realization of your Self as the omniscient Seer of all.

Time is not a concern for the yogi. Your Self is eternal, so you have all the time you need. However, you may find that embodied living becomes much more enjoyable as your consciousness becomes clearer, your mind stronger and your realization of Self-knowledge becomes more pronounced. So why not start now, wherever you are on the spectrum of realization, and do your best with the process?

Self-inquiry will yield the best results once you are able to practice the last four limbs of yoga, but there is no reason to wait that long. You can begin to wonder and contemplate the nature of your Self at any time. Even a few minutes of Self-reflection throughout the day will initiate the process. It will even help you meditate better during your intensive practice sessions. We will explore this process in the chapter on contemplation.

For now, when you have a moment of free time, simply wonder what you are. Think about your personality. Think about the dreams you had last night. Think about all of your likes and dislikes. Think about how you saw the world when you were five years old. Then wonder, "Who or what was it that witnessed all of these experiences?" The more often you do this, you will begin to see a thread of consciousness that ties together, or maybe it is better to say runs through, each of these experiences. That is you. The stronger that realization and the direct experience of this truth becomes in your everyday awareness, the closer you are to complete Self-realization.

A year after beginning Kriya Yoga practice, I was introduced to the concept of Self-inquiry through Dr. David Frawley's book *Vedantic Meditation: Lighting the Flame of Awareness*. I don't remember much about the book, other than it got me wondering, "What am I?" This then led me to discover the work of Ramana Maharshi.

I was in my very early 20s and overzealous. Luckily, my wife was patient. I took note cards and wrote the following phrases: "Who Am I?", "Who sees this?", "What am I?" and "Who is aware of this experience?". Our small apartment was covered with the yellow note cards. One was on the refrigerator. One, I placed on the cabinet door, knowing I would see it every morning when I made tea. I put these little notes anywhere I thought I would see them regularly. I even put one on the toilet so I would think long and hard about "Who was aware of this experience?" She was very happy when I outgrew the note cards as training aids. And when our friends and family came to visit, they no longer thought I had gone crazy.

However silly I was being, it was good for me at that time. It kept my mind focused on sincere curiosity about what I was, in relationship to this idea of a Self that is eternal and beyond conception. I would practice my Kriya meditation routine twice a day. At other times, when I was engaged in my regular life activities, I was often reminded to take a moment and reflect on the nature of the Self. This kept me focused and engaged.

As my ability to focus and meditations naturally lengthened, I began to include five to 15 minutes of specific contemplation on the phrase "Who or what am I?" at the end of each Kriya practice. This was very rewarding. To this day, I spend a considerable time reflecting on Self-knowledge throughout my meditations, both for myself and for others. This occurs while I am practicing Kriya, or if I am sitting quietly, without a particular technique in action.

Remember, the final limbs of Kriya Yoga are those of concentration, meditation and the experience of oneness. If we concentrate, rest our awareness on and experience cognitive absorption with the Self, we are Self-realized. When that absorption realization with Self is permanent, whether we are meditating, contemplating or otherwise, this is the ultimate maturation of spiritual practice. Our work of Kriya and knowledge from Vichara bears its final fruit, and we are supremely free, as we are meant to be.

Now the knowledge of Vichara is most important. It is knowledge that removes the spiritually dangerous obstacles of hope and belief. And, as we have seen from the above description, Kriya is the perfect vehicle for refining our temporal manifestation to explore the knowledge of our being, which is essentially the knowledge of our universe. The more knowledgeable we are about our capacities, capabilities and reality, the less we cling to hopes and belief. The less we cling to hopes and beliefs, the easier we can see consciousness as it is, and ourselves for what we truly are.

Why are hopes and beliefs dangerous? Hope is based on the wish that something or someone is a certain way. We do not have knowledge. Rather than seeking out the truth of that thing or person, we merely hope. What we hope for may coincidentally turn out to be correct. Yet, it is better to simply wait and see how something is going to turn out, rather than to hope for an occurrence that is not based on knowledge. When we take the effort to seek and find knowledge, we know. There is no need for hope, and we can then make peace with the reality. When there is this peace, there is not the danger of being harmed by hopes that fail to meet our expectations.

Belief, like hope, is another way to avoid seeking out or experiencing the truth of a situation. It is hope and belief that make us cling to ideas, situations and activities that may be a complete waste of time. It is belief that tells us if we chant 186,000 mantras, the Goddess of Fortune will be pleased with us. In reality, it is only wasting our vital life force in an obsessive-compulsive delusion, because we don't want to face the fact that we just don't want to learn the rules for successful financial health.

It is belief that drives us to see problems with our fellow humans. We believe we are right and they are wrong. We believe we know best, and they do not. This causes conflict and strife. If we had the courage to take the time to see that all our needs are ultimately the same, we would not denigrate those walking a different path.

We believe we are unworthy of knowing the God or the Self, and so that belief keeps us acting as though we are separate. If we could quiet our mind, and contemplate our relationship to God and Self until full realization dawned, we would then act appropriately in knowledge, and not out of false beliefs. It is the practice of Kriya that quiets the mind. It is the practice of Vichara that allows us the capacity to contemplate and gain knowledge directly.

When we have knowledge, we do not need belief or hope. When we know the Self and that we are never separate from it, that we are it, we don't have to affirm it every day, 108 times a day during a meditation.

This is why preparing the foundation through the work of Kriya, to realize the knowledge of our being is, as Vasistha says, "the means to liberation." When you have knowledge, you are certain. When you are certain, you are at peace. When you are peace, you are free to explore the depths, shallows and infinity of your being. When you know this holistic latitude of your consciousness, you are free. Then, the shallow end of the pool is no more or less inviting then the deep end. It is all water.

-

Many people who read this kind of book are spiritual seekers. They identify with the spiritual path as good and holy. This may not be true for all, but many will see anyone living a life that is not devoted to spiritual seeking as a complete waste of time. I would like to encourage you to think on the contrary. A life that is only devoted to spiritual seeking, instead of living, is the waste of time. It is like a person who undertakes fitness training, only so they can undertake more fitness training. You train yourself to give yourself the capacity to joyfully undertake an experience.

A mountain climber trains not to keep training to climb a mountain, but so he or she can actually go climb that mountain. A gardener learns about flowers and seasons, and does the work tilling the earth and planting seeds so she can see the lovely light of the Self in all the summer blossoms. All things in life require work, knowledge and then the opportunity to experience the fruits of the process. It is what God does through each of us.

Do not be a spiritual seeker. Be one who is training to live freely and wholly. The real purpose of meditation and inquiry and all the rest of it is so you can live freely as your infinite being, beyond desire, craving, hope and limitation. Once you train to the point where you have the knowledge that this is true, you then have to LIVE as though it is true. You must

LIVE the adventure of your life. This adventure continues forever, whether you are in the physical realm, astral or causal realm. As I learned during one of my first cosmic consciousness experiences, "THERE IS NO END TO IT!" For this reason, do not try to escape this world. For there is nothing to escape and nowhere to go. There is only the manifestation of your consciousness in its present state. Once you master your consciousness, if you don't like the present state, you can either wait for it to change, or shift it yourself.

Do not be one who says, "I want to be liberated so I can get off of this planet!" The reason you want to get off this planet has nothing to do with spiritual liberation. If you were liberated, you would not mind too much, wherever you happened to be. You long to escape, because there is something in your life that is painful. Deal with that directly. The more skillful you become at managing and resolving the little problems in your life, the better suited you will be to tackle the bigger questions of your existence. Not until then. If you are in pain now, and do not deal with the underlying cause, your karma will follow you, and you will have other reasons to experience pain elsewhere.

The goal I put before you is not to glorify and try to be a person who can sit transfixed for hours on a hard floor, in perfect stillness untouched by the sorrows of this world, or be the image of a perfect saint with love and devotion for all. I challenge you to master your consciousness, to be your Self, and to master the unique role Self plays through your personality. I challenge you to undertake the necessary disciplines to prepare your mind to fully absorb itself in the truth of its endless being. Then I challenge you to give yourself the opportunity to maintain that knowledge of the Self, whether sitting at home in meditation, or fully engaged in the maelstrom of everyday living.

In this way, if you are naturally directed to be a self-absorbed hermit yogi, you can be. If you are naturally directed to be an extroverted businessperson, you can be — but not out of compulsion, or because it's the right thing to do, but because it is natural for your unique expression of the divine on this earth.

No matter what your natural expression, it is not the external manifestation that matters. It is the internal knowledge of the Self, which never waivers or dims, that is the true mark of realized being. And no one will ever know that but you. This is the way of yoga. This is the result of Vichara (Self-inquiry) supported by Kriya (yogic techniques).

Chapter Two

ADVANCED SPIRITUALITY

You are taking the first steps to realizing the greatest work of humankind. The same fortitude, focus, concentration, dedication, patience, discipline and devotion to complete this task is known only to such people at the top tier of their professions. Consider world-class Olympians, surgeons, musicians, self-made millionaires, stay-at-home mothers, and military specialists or similar successful individuals. Consider the time and perseverance required for their success. If your longing to know your Self, to know your true relationship to the divine, is as motivating as the drive and ambition of the world's most successful people, you will succeed.

If you have the capacity to make the personal sacrifices, to endure the tedious inner work, to get up day after day, and year after year, to master your consciousness without any promise of glory or acknowledgement from the world, then you will succeed. If you are willing to seek out spiritual experts when you need them, avoid the grandiose claims of those who promise an easy, quick method, and acknowledge it will be your own Self-effort that completes the task of Self-realization, you will be successful. (Always remember, grace and Self-effort are synonymous.)

Through the eons, your consciousness has been changing, evolving, awakening out of a long slumber. You have experienced the consciousness of rocks, plants, mountains, trees, lakes, insects, reptiles and mammals. You have been humans who cared only for violence and petty fortunes. You have been great men and women, as well as the lowest beggar and thief. Throughout each experience, your consciousness has been maturing. Like an oak grows from a seed to a sapling and into a great awesome tree, your consciousness has been expanding.

The maturation can be seen in the development of a healthy human being. At first, there is no sense of self, only a body that eats, sleeps and eliminates. As time passes, the child realizes it has needs and can get those needs met. The ego develops and with it comes craving and desires. As the child matures into an adult, a sense of duty and dedication to something greater may dawn — not always, but it might. In the proper environment, the human consciousness will then blossom free of the mortal concerns it had as a dutiful adult and release itself into the contemplation of the greater mysteries. When death comes, it is prepared. It has grown through this particular stage and now enters the next.

Most people in the current era can be seen to exist in the consciousness of a child, only searching to have its cravings and desires fulfilled. Some will be at the level of duty and dedication to society and humankind in general. Few will truly consider the mysteries and prepare themselves for the next phase of consciousness.

There is no judgment in this. It is natural. It is as silly to judge a two-year-old for throwing a tantrum as it is to judge anyone at their current stage of development. It is just as useful to condemn an oak seed for not being a tree as it is to expect anyone to be anything other than what they are. It is a continuum that we all must go through.

So you see, human consciousness is a stage, a step in the greater process of the universe. The stage of exploring meditation and yoga sincerely is just part of the recipe required to complete the maturation process of consciousness. You are now at, or close to that stage.

As with all endeavors, there are plenty of ways to complete the task. There are plenty of pitfalls, plenty of fantasies to avoid, and plenty of help, as well. The method you have chosen is that of Kriya Yoga and Self-inquiry. One prepares you for the other. Both together provide all the tools and structure necessary for success in the realization of Self-knowledge.

Although there will be plenty of moments of ecstasy and peace, actualizing this process will not always be easy, nor will it always be enjoyable. Yet once realized, it is the most fulfilling undertaking you ever could have hoped to be engaged in. If this is acceptable, then let us begin…

The Self, the undivided infinite consciousness, is ever present and timeless. It is simultaneously the objects of experience, the capacity to experience, and the witness of all phenomena. It is both the ever-changing world of form and the changeless being in which the world of form rises and falls. It is the work of Kriya Yoga to reveal this reality through direct experience.

Spiritual practice returns our capacity to exist in and as a pure being, allowing us to know our infinite existence, while relating appropriately to the world of form. The world of form includes the roles we have chosen to play in time and space, and the temporary imagined limitations required to play those roles. Spiritual practice enables us to reconcile our infinite being with our temporal form. A spiritually advanced individual can withdraw attention into the pure being of Self in meditation as easily as he or she can live a normal, unassuming life.

Pain, suffering and confusion can arise if all we can perceive is the ever-changing phenomena of the limited existence of our current personality and life situation. It is like being trapped in a dream. When we dream, we often forget that we are the dreamer and every person, place and thing we see, feel, touch, hear and smell within the dream is a projection of our own consciousness. When a dreamer becomes lucid, the dream is experienced for what it is, a play of the many and varied components of consciousness that have been accumulated or created while engaged in time and space. A lucid dream loses its sense of immediacy, because the dreamer then sees everything clearly and in perspective.

Kriya Yoga does not make life better. It gives proper perspective on what life is. Kriya Yoga removes the obstacles that allow us to see the Self-shining nature of spirit in all people, places, times and circumstances. When this is obvious, stress, pain and frustration melt into contentment, peace, love and knowledge.

To make life better may require a shift in attitude, a change of associations, counseling to deal with unresolved trauma and mental stress or a change in diet and lifestyle routines. All of these actions are supports for our advanced spiritual practice. They enable us to derive the full benefit of an intensive and intelligent application of the Kriya Yoga techniques and principles.

The teachings within this book assume that you have either successfully dealt with the mundane problems of your life or are actively working on them and are at the point where they cease to be a distraction. Self-realization requires energy, dedication, discipline and time. The more of that we have to dedicate to our inner work, the quicker will be the results.

WHAT IS ADVANCED SPIRITUALITY?

Advanced spirituality does not require more and better techniques. It does not require extensive philosophical debate or the knowledge of exotic and foreign words. It simply requires that one understand the basic mechanisms that lead to inner stillness, and then have the courage to explore the nature of consciousness and being.

Advanced spirituality also requires that we understand the purpose of spirituality. By this, I mean that we are not sublimating unresolved psychological needs into the socially acceptable outlet of religion. Instead, we are approaching the Kriya practices and techniques with their actual purpose in mind — to know the wholeness of life and being and our relationship to it and as it.

In regards to the mechanism of spiritual growth, remember all meditation and spiritual practices have one thing in common. They encourage a practitioner to learn how to focus attention and hold attention in one place. This can occur through mindfulness, focusing on a mantra, divine chanting, Hatha Yoga practice, pranayama, profound contemplation or any number of possible variations. The core principle is the capacity to concentrate and hold consciousness in one place.

It is also important that this capacity to concentrate translates across all activities. I mention this because often people ask me questions, such as, "If I am sewing, and I'm fully involved in my work, doesn't that count as meditation?" or "When I go rock climbing, I'm fully in the zone and aware of nothing else, does that count?" My answer is typically, "No." This is because these experiences do not allow a person to experience stillness unless they are engaged in that specific activity. The yogic processes of meditation, when practiced regularly, reveal that stillness into all of our activities, whether we are racing down a mountainside, sleeping, working, cooking dinner, meditating or having a conversation.

Also, meditation and yogic concentration allow us to direct our attention within, releasing all attachments to those things we find so important in daily life. Only when we have released attachment to our transient personality and life situation can we fully contemplate and identify with transcendental reality.

Once the capacity to focus and maintain focus has been developed, a person can then ignore distractions or the constant barrage of old karmic impressions. The longer one can remain peacefully internalized while letting karmic impressions exhaust themselves, the quicker karma becomes less influential in daily life. We will discuss how this occurs later in this text.

In time, we can remain internalized and then contemplate questions, such as, "Where does karma come from?", "Who or what am I, really?", "Is this pain (or joy) real?", "How does this world of form arise?", "What was I before I was born?", etc. From this capacity to exist internalized in stillness, and then to contemplate our spiritual questions until direct knowing dawns, is the direct way to an enlightened consciousness.

In this text, we will cover all Kriya meditation and pranayama procedures I have been initiated into and have practiced every day since beginning this path. These practices will enable you to free your consciousness from the karmic impressions of the mind, to master your inner consciousness, and to contemplate all of your spiritual questions until direct knowledge dawns. The emphasis will be on understanding and applying the mechanics of what makes the practices work, rather than striving for more complexity or esoteric methods. Advanced spirituality requires proper intention and the capacity to harness the simple and obvious procedures effectively, rather than striving for an ideal promoted by individuals who capitalize on complex or esoteric yogic methods.

TAKING A SELF-INVENTORY

There are questions to ask yourself to determine your readiness to begin practicing Kriya Yoga. If you can answer "Yes" to these questions, you are ready to begin or deepen your advanced spiritual work. If you answer "No" to any of these questions, take some time to contemplate what you need to do so that your answer changes to "Yes." Do not despair if you do answer negatively. Whatever activities are required to answer all of the questions below affirmatively is also Kriya Yoga practice.

The questions are:

1) Am I at a place in my life where I can schedule regular interludes of quiet reflective meditation and spiritual study throughout the day, every day, without distraction?

Life can sometimes be hectic, dramatic and distracting. This can occur due to our own choices or from unconscious karmic impressions of which we are not aware. The choices we make in the present are always the most important. They determine our future. It is the actions, thoughts and affirmations we held in the past that determine our present. By consistently making choices that allow you to have a well-organized daily schedule where you can meditate and study without distraction will eventually result in a life situation where you have ample time for meditation and reflection. Be firm in your decision and let go of attachments to people, places, situations or circumstances that do not support your intention.

2) Are my relationships healthy and drama free?

The people we relate to in life are a reflection of our inner states of consciousness. This is one reason why the idea of keeping the company of holy people is such a strong theme in yogic traditions. By holy people, we are simply referring to people who have silent minds, clear states of consciousness and are aware of their true nature. We are not implying or encouraging any kind of guru worship or deification. Anyone who exhibits the above traits falls into the category of "holy." More will be said on this in the chapter on The Four Gatekeepers of Liberation.

As a Kriya Yogi, it is your responsibility either to remove the people from your life who constantly distract you or cause you drama, or remove yourself from the relationship. You are not responsible for them. If you choose a drama-free path of silent meditation and they are not interested, cannot respect or support it, that is their choice. It is best to move on. You will not find much success in meditation if your mind is filled with incessant thoughts about relationships that do not inspire peace.

3) Is my financial situation stable, or at least are all of my resources realistically and responsibly provided for so I do not have to dwell on monetary problems?

In the past, it was often advised for those interested in pursuing spiritual work to give up dependence on finances and renounce material things. This is understandable. Nothing can be more stressful than money troubles. However, times have changed. As Lahiri Mahasaya has said and demonstrated, our renunciation needs to be internal and not obvious. If we are truly fully functional mature beings, we have the capacity to provide for our basic needs. By doing so, we maintain a consciousness of renunciation by not becoming attached to or defining ourselves through our gains.

There is work to be done while in this world. There is no need to be a beggar. If we know that all is the one divine infinite consciousness, what difference does it make to have a career and fulfill mundane responsibilities?

Also remember that if you follow your bliss, money doesn't always follow, particularly if you have a poor business plan, feel that you must absolutely love your work all of the time, or do not know the laws of having and managing money well. Do what you need to in a surrendered fashion, to have enough resources for a safe dwelling, transportation and healthy food. This is also Kriya Yoga practice. Renunciation isn't about getting rid of everything and every responsibility. It is about fulfilling your responsibilities without attachment. When this is done, it is easy to turn our attention within without distraction during meditation.

4) Have I done all that I can to have and maintain a healthy body?

Proper diet, healthy exercise, regular sleep schedules and a balance of rest, activity and recreation are essential to Kriya practice. It is the body and nervous system that act as receptacle and transmitter of our inner consciousness so long as the body lives. The healthier we are, the easier it will be for us to relate to and interact with consciousness in this realm.

Some health problems may be congenital or genetic. We may have to live with certain bodily imperfections. That is part of life. However, we can do our best to have the healthiest body possible without being obsessive. I mention this only because many interested in the field of spirituality and yoga become so obsessed with diet, lifestyle and health that they forget that our purpose is not to perfect the body for its own sake, but only so that we can meditate, contemplate and live as freely as possible. Unless you are a professional athlete, your focus on health should be on a long healthy life, and not on bodily glorification for its own sake.

5) Am I psychologically healthy? Have I dealt with and discarded any addictive, obsessive or compulsive behaviors?

If you have known psychological disturbances, find the proper treatment to resolve or minimize them. Often people will come to spiritual practice thinking they will be healed or cured of psychic or psychological disturbances. That is not the role of advanced spirituality. If you are not healthy minded or relatively sane, your mental perversions or insanity will find a new expression in your spiritual path. Consider all of the "spiritual" people who are fanatical, or who feel it is their mission to find fault with the paths of others, rather than attending to their own private spiritual work while radiating a consciousness of peace in the world.

6) Do I respect everyone's spiritual journey without judgment?

Believe it or not, even people on the Kriya path consistently find fault with their brother and sister practitioners. There are many lineages and branches of Kriya yoga. Lahiri Mahasaya had many students he authorized to teach. Sri Yukteswar, Lahiri Mahasaya's student, also had at least two well-known disciples. Paramahansa Yogananda, Sri Yukteswar's student, even authorized both known and unknown students to teach Kriya practices. This will continue so long as there is life in the Kriya tradition. The different branches of the Kriya lineage may not agree on everything, but individuals always find the proper lineage for themselves.

While this question is really intended to encourage you to consider respecting all spiritual teachings and traditions, even if you do not understand them, I would also like you to extend this courtesy to all of your brother and sister Kriya yogis, no matter their lineage. Finding fault with others' practices takes energy away from your own personal private practice.

7) Am I not driven to practice Kriya Yoga because I want to feel like I belong somewhere or to be accepted by people who share similar beliefs?

Ultimately, Kriya practice is about realizing the truth about your concepts of the divine, learning who you are at the core of your being and living from that knowing. If you are lonely, or looking for people with similar beliefs, your intentions may be misguided. It is better to find a hobby and join a club rather than look to Kriya as a pastime to fulfill your social deficits.

More will be said on this later.

8) Is my only motivation to know the full and complete Self-realization?

This is the only motivation that will give complete results of Kriya practice.

9) Am I realistic about spiritual development, knowing that it takes months, years and decades to understand the subtle intricacies and to grow into full spiritual maturity? Am I fully committed, no matter how long it might take?

If you have read *Autobiography of a Yogi*, you are familiar with the fantastic stories, the exuberance of Paramahansa Yogananda and the amazing promises that are contained within that text. These are wonderful and inspiring. That is the purpose of that book, to inspire you.

What most people miss within those pages is what went on behind the scenes to make Yogananda's life such a spiritual inspiration. He began meditating when he was a child. He meditated every day. He turned his energy from schoolwork, from having a family, from most all distractions until he experienced union with and realization of his divine concept.

This process took years of intensive dedication. It was not because of any magic from his guru or any specialness on Yogananda's part, unless you consider his single-minded devotion unique. You, too, can mature through the levels of awakening, if you are patient and willing to follow the same steps as it relates to your own personal expression. This may offend devotees of that great yogi, and that is not my intention. If Yogananda were asked to confirm the truth of these thoughts, don't you think he would do so? Did he not admit that everyone had the capacity to attain Self and God realization?

I am not saying that you must act like Yogananda. I am only saying you must do what he did as it relates to your own life path. Minimize distractions, turn your energy and attention to your spiritual practice and surrender to the process.

I am putting an emphasis on considering questions or ideas in the first two chapters of this book. My reasoning is to make sure we are clear on what is required to progress through Kriya Yoga practice and that your intention and goal is nothing other than Self-realization.

FALSE IDEAS TO BE DISCARDED

As advanced Kriya practitioners, there are many false ideas we must overcome or see through. This is mainly due to the fact that most people seeking to practice Kriya Yoga, or any spiritual quickening procedure, are not actually looking to be Self-realized. They are looking to find an escape from pain, or are looking for a group to belong to because they are lonely or misunderstood, or they are looking to have an absent mother or father figure replaced with a guru or a loving concept of the divine. This is understandable.

It is the natural drive of being human to seek fulfillment and bliss. But eternal bliss and freedom cannot ever be derived from aversion to the hardship of life, or by belonging to a group that makes us feel special or important, or by hoping to have the acceptance and love of a parental figure. These motivations can serve to get us on the path, but they cannot actually carry us to true bliss, the realization of the Self and the knowledge and experience of our timeless eternal nature. Rather than look to Kriya practice to resolve issues as mentioned above, it is better to seek professional counseling. Then Kriya practice can be fully reserved for balancing the nervous system, harmonizing the energetic and astral channels and profound contemplation.

Consider the idea of marriage. If we come into a marriage with the desire to complete ourselves through partnership then our motivations are not pure. We hope to get something from the marriage, and that which we hope to achieve is completion. This reveals the fact that we feel incomplete. However, if we come into a marriage to enjoy the opportunity to support our partner and to have an outlet for our devotion and love, then the marriage is a vehicle for amplifying our love and devotion. It is not based on attachment or idea of incompleteness. This concept can be related to our spiritual practice as well.

Approaching spiritual practice to avoid pain is of a tamasic nature. Approaching spiritual practice to change or improve ourself is of a rajasic nature. Approaching a spiritual practice for the simple love and joy of doing so is of a sattvic nature. (These terms are described in the previous book *Kriya Yoga: Continuing the Lineage of Enlightenment*.) We may go through stages before we reach the sattvic (serene or Self-fulfilling) state of practice, but eventually that must be the only reason we meditate, pray, chant or contemplate, for the sheer joy of doing so. This is the only reason that will fully ignite our spiritual realizations. It must be done for no other purpose than the sheer joy of it.

By committing to a spiritual path because we feel incomplete or inferior, we are affirming that something outside of ourselves can provide this completion or sense of worthiness. This will never be true. When we approach a spiritual path under these conditions, we are more prone to create situations that further bind us, rather than liberate us. It is more likely we will get involved with teachers or organizations that do not care about our liberation, but seek the expansion of the organization or deification (sometimes subtle, sometimes obvious) of the teacher. We are also more prone to fall under subtle manipulation. This can seem harmless enough, and it probably is in mundane terms, but nothing will stall Self-realization quicker than giving up one's power and capacity to be rational to a person or organization that admits to having our best interest at heart. Some organizations and teachers are healthy and helpful. Some are not. The quality of devotees they generate and attract is the best assessing factor.

This does not mean that we are to avoid people who may be able to help us or guide us. It means we have to take responsibility for our own path. It means we have to maintain a healthy dose of respectful skepticism. It means we must remain alert and perceptive about those we choose to learn from, and the advice that is given.

If we are given faulty advice (spiritual or otherwise), do not automatically follow it, simply because the advisor is a respected person. Pay attention to the results of the advice. Listen to the advisors who most often give supportive or worthwhile advice. Give yourself permission to let go of attachment to those who may mean well, but are not helpful. This is also part of the path.

By taking responsibility for our own path, we are admitting that there may be people who know more than we do or have more experience. We are willing to learn from them. Yet we are not expecting that their state of consciousness, thoughts or actions can do anything extraordinary for us. No authentic teacher in this era will claim or imply such capacity. An authentic teacher can point the way, describe what has worked for them, but they leave your own work up to you. They let you find and cultivate your own spiritual bliss and knowledge.

Respectful skepticism means that we do not blindly believe everything we hear from someone who seems important or who has a level of status in the world (spiritually or otherwise) or comes from a respected lineage. Fame and being well known has nothing to do with capacity, wisdom or skill. If we do find ourselves drawn to a particular teacher or teaching, it is our duty to not get drawn into it until we have actually verified the principles being shared. If a teaching is found to be wanting, then let it go and move on.

There is no need to judge. Only admit that just because someone comes from a lineage that is famous or claims to have special knowledge does not mean they do. There are just as many frauds in the spiritual scene as there are in any other field. Having a large following or many influential members to an organization is also not a proper gauge of authenticity. Pay attention to all the organizations of the world, both spiritual and secular, and you can see how this is true. A teacher's authenticity may be reflected in applicable wisdom, capacity to admit their faults, inner calm, ability to share spiritual procedures that work and an unassuming nature.

If you find a teaching that is logical, provides a clear path for Self-exploration and discovery, does not require any oaths or pacts, does not make any outrageous promises and is realistic about the amount of Self-effort and work required to experience spiritual growth, it is worth pursuing. Teachings and teachers who are interested in your liberation of consciousness do not shy away from a student's healthy skepticism. They do not give advice about what a student "should" do. Nor do they require any special commitments, other than the promise to create a life that supports one's spiritual work and the dedication to practice and explore what is taught until full Self-realization dawns.

After we find proper guidance and instruction, and have taken the practical steps to resolve any physical, emotional, mental or psychological issues that may delay our capacity to meditate and contemplate well we are ready to devote our time and energy to advanced Kriya practice. Through our pure devotion, free of the motivations caused by attraction and aversion, we can gain clear insights and understanding into the nature of our Self and its relationship to our concepts of reality. Through this direct experience, we are liberated.

Kriya Yoga practice will not change the world. Through your practice and the practice of others, there may be greater harmony between peoples, but the world has its own destiny. The world of form will continue to evolve and improve as our solar system moves through the galaxy towards the galactic center. As the ages continue to ascend, so will the capacity of human consciousness on this planet. It is a natural process and does not require your participation or validation.

The current conditions of collective consciousness are such to fulfill the karmas of the souls who have incarnated at this time. You have incarnated at this point in history because your inner states of consciousness resonate with the current trends of the collective consciousness. Through your Kriya practice you can, in time, release your Self from the karmic bonds that attach you to this space-time continuum. You can also release your Self from the karmic bonds that will require you to incarnate again in future generations. The point of spiritual practice is not to improve the world or even your physical self, but to realize what you truly are in relationship to the world of form. Once fully conscious with this knowledge, you can choose to incarnate in any time or space, or not at all.

Similarly, you cannot change anyone through your Kriya practice. If you feel an inspiration to save other people's souls through your Kriya practice, or you think that by teaching them Kriya, you will save them pain and suffering, you are misguided. The work that needs to be done, spiritually speaking, is your own release from attachments and removal of ignorance, which prevents you from seeing and being what you are. Once this is accomplished, you are done and you are ready for whatever realms and adventures await you.

When the time is right, every soul will turn towards the appropriate path for them. They will then realize the truth of their being and they will be happy. Until that time comes, every soul has their own specific karma to work through and understand. No one and no thing can change that. Our paths are personal, and all revelations come in their appropriate time, when the soul is ready. To be concerned about others salvation is to avoid the responsibility of your own hard work that is necessary to awaken.

When you have direct experience of your infinite timeless nature and can maintain your consciousness in that realization, you will see directly that this is so and you will not worry about "other" people. You will see each state of consciousness as a perfectly orchestrated wholeness, and that the ideas of good, bad, salvation, liberation and bondage were all part of a rather complex and interesting game. I know this can be a hard concept to entertain at first, especially with all the suffering and hardship in the world. Do not take my word for it. Practice and see.

SUBTLE ASPECTS OF ADVANCED KRIYA PRACTICE

When Yogananda brought Kriya Yoga practice to the West, he entered a culture dominated by Christianity and other traditional American values of that time. He couched his teachings in such a way as to fit the society. This is why there is such a strong devotional and Christian sentiment throughout his work. This is also why the majority of his work is more churchlike than yogic. This was appropriate for the introduction of Kriya into the West.

As the century passed, meditation and yoga became more en vogue. It was then most appropriate to focus on the teachings as a means for stress-management and health. This is why, even today, the subtler aspects of Kriya practice (and yoga in general) are not practiced or readily understood. This is as it should be.

The focus was first on establishing the tradition, then turned to the practical value of meditation and yoga. This process has successfully preserved the seed of Kriya so that it may culturally blossom into its full potential. Many may have already discovered or been inwardly guided towards the full potential of Kriya. This book is not for them. This book is for those who need further or more concrete clarification of the process.

It is one thing to practice Kriya pranayama until we reach inner tranquility or Jyoti Mudra until we can actually see the light in the third eye center, but what then? How do we dynamically engage these experiences to quicken and complete our spiritual realization? Once we master the mechanics, then we can explore the dynamics that lead to unqualified Self-realization. These methods will be described in the chapters dealing with technique.

The techniques of Kriya Yoga Vichara include mudra, mantra, pranayama, concentration and various threads of contemplation. Each technique has a role in harmonizing our physiology, balancing the energetic pathways of the body, cleansing the astral body and enabling direct experience of certain states of consciousness necessary to fully actualize consistent and stable Self-realization. Even when only practiced mechanically, the techniques are excellent stress- reduction tools. When practiced dynamically and with attention, Kriya Yoga techniques rapidly quicken our capacity to experience Self and Divine Realization.

This quickening of Divine Realization occurs because the Kriya processes have the capacity to reveal and dissolve the interior veils that prevent us from perceiving the complete reality of what we are beyond name, thought and form. Consider a person who is trying to interact with the world around them. Imagine this person is wearing earmuffs, dark and cracked eyeglasses, and thick rubber gloves. Interacting with the world wearing these kinds of apparatus will not allow the person to accurately perceive her environment. The apparatus must be taken off and cast aside, so that one's senses can fully appreciate the true reality of the world. As we perfect our spiritual techniques, they have the same effect of removing the energetic, mental and psychological conditioning that prevents our clear perception and experience of consciousness.

This process may not always be easy. We know from the Bhagavad Gita, an allegory explaining the soul's (Arjuna) path to awakened consciousness (Krishna), that in the beginning we may be overwhelmed by the perceived difficulty of the task of spiritual growth. In the Gita, when Arjuna perceives that he will have to slay his kinsmen (comfortable psychological habits and tendencies), he loses his motivation. This is illustrated by him dropping his bow (giving up on meditation) and collapsing onto his chariot (shirking his spiritual duty).

Krishna (a representation of our enlightened consciousness) then responds, "From where has this weakness come to you at this difficult time? It is not befitting you who are of noble character. It does not lead to the state of spiritual fulfillment, and can only cause disgrace. Yield not to this immature behavior; it is not suitable for you. Abandon this show of weakness and faintheartedness. Stand up, Arjuna!"

Our psychological habits and tendencies are what form the structure of who we think we are as a personality. The Kriya process, paired with Vichara, reveals that we are not the personality, and the personality is only a point of awareness through which a greater consciousness breathes. We are called to slay (remove our attention from) those psychological habits and tendencies so that we can fully perceive the totality of our enlightened being. We can only experience this enlightened being when we are free from the bonds of psychological conditioning that made us think we are only a small personality with a limited history.

It can be hard to let this go. It takes faith and trust. Imagine someone says to you, "If you jump off that cliff, I guarantee you will be able to fly." The same feelings arise when a Self-realized teacher says, "If you completely and totally let go of your personality and history, you will experience unencumbered spiritual clarity." We don't believe it. We can't imagine it, because we've never done it before (within memory).

The Kriya processes and Self-inquiry methodically give us direct experiences of what it is like to loosen the bonds to our personality and history. Then, once we have developed enough skill in the practices and accumulated enough evidence, we can say, "Maybe it is true that if I release my attachment to my personality and history I will know spiritual freedom." We can take that final leap of faith, and truly surrender to our greater consciousness.

This is the result of the subtle aspects of our Kriya Yoga Vichara practice. Those subtle aspects are not about churning out more Kriya pranayamas, or spending more time reciting the phrase "Who am I" for hours on end. The subtle practice is utilizing the methods of Kriya technique and Self-inquiry to consciously and with attention examine your attachment to useless psychological conditioning and memory. It requires that once you are calm and clear, to truly contemplate "What is this I-sensation that is felt while I sit here in meditation?" That contemplation is beyond thinking. It requires learning to feel the I-sensation and see how it relates to your every experience through and beyond time.

How this occurs will be different for everyone. The mechanism that initiates the process can be the same, such as engaging Kriya pranayama and contemplating the source of the I-thought. Yet how the realization unfolds will be specific to each unique manifestation of God's individualized consciousness.

In Chapter 11 of the *Bhagavad Gita*, after Krishna (Our Own Fully Enlightened Consciousnes) reveals his complete divine manifestation (Reality) to Arjuna (A symbol for all who would seek God), Krishna states, "By grace, by my own power, this supreme form has been shown to you; my form of splendor, which is universal, infinite, and primal, which has never before been seen by anyone but you." In this statement, he reveals the unique divine realization that will be different for all of us, even though the effect will be the same.

This is one reason why it is important to avoid talking about your realizations with other seekers. It is none of their business and usually when we talk about spiritual experiences, it is only to validate the reality of what we have realized. Your realizations cannot be validated by projecting them into the lives of others. Your realizations are deeply personal.

Also, having a conversation with another seeker cannot help you. If they are still seeking, then they are not the people to seek counsel from. Learn from someone who has accomplished a task, not from someone who is still figuring it out! If neither you nor your friend knew how to build a house, yet that was your desire, would you ask your friend how it's done? No. You would find an accomplished builder and say, "Show me how to make this work." The realization path is no different.

Many people begin the path of Self-realization only to quickly give it up, or to continue, but only out of an obsessive-compulsive ritual. The seeker who gives up usually does so because it becomes clear that there is more to the process than the mechanical repetition of technique. They start to experience the inner changes and it scares them, because it will require that they shift how they experience reality.

The seeker may start to realize that God is not a caring personality that gives out blessings or sits with angels in heaven surrounded by divine masters of old, but a direct and intimate foundation for the totality of every experience. The seeker may start to understand what is truly meant when a long dead enlightened master is quoted to have said, "When you think of me I will be near to help you." They realize it is not that a disembodied holy being is taking a personal interest in their welfare. They realize that by attuning to an idea (the master's name and form) that is associated with clarity of consciousness, that helps their own present experience resonate with that same clarity.

These realizations can be overwhelming to one who is not ready to grow to emotional maturity. It is easier to believe the comfortable fantasy rather than the clear reality. This is why I highly recommend one not begin these practices unless they are already psychologically healthy and balanced. If you are prone to fantasy and delusion, spiritual practice may only exacerbate that problem.

Many people seek spiritual practice to heal their life situations or to make them happy. This is a good sentiment, but that is not the purpose of yoga practice. Yoga practice is for the purpose of unqualified spiritual freedom. It is not about healing situations. It is for a giving direct experience of reality beyond myopic identification with the mind, history, name and form of the world. Once we are relatively psychologically balanced and mentally emotionally mature, we have greater capacity to grow beyond our concepts and expectations of what we think spiritual practice should be. We are ready to accept what it actually is. This is a beautiful way to begin.

To fully engage the subtle and advanced processes of Kriya Yoga Vichara mandates that we are willing to grow beyond our spiritual concepts. This requires the courage to confront our psychological complexes and the faith to embrace the awe and grace of that which cannot be known or described. It requires the courage and curiosity to embrace that which is free of concepts. Can you imagine it? Perhaps you cannot, but I encourage you to try. The trying will lead to the experience which no imagination can envision.

ENLIGHTENMENT IS NOT WHAT WE THINK

It is a difficult thing to imagine what prevents us from experiencing reality directly. Using the analogy of the dream once more, remember how real a dream seems while it is happening. Remember how there is usually absolutely no concept available in a dream in reference to your actual waking life. It is as if you are in an entirely different world, with an entirely different cast of characters, and that place and those people are all you know and all you've ever known. No matter how strange or odd the dream is, everything somehow makes sense in dreamtime. The dreamer rarely ever thinks, "This isn't right!" or "That floating table with the burning water doesn't make any sense!"

Our waking life is very similar to the dream, although it does seem more consistent. There are things we believe or accept that may or may not be true. Some beliefs or concepts are so strong, yet like the dream, are really only applicable to our personal waking-dream experience. How can this be realized? How can we know what is true? How can we face and see through our misperceptions and illusions? It is the spiritual practices of the world that serve to shake us out of our personal dreams. They are also mechanisms of the dream, otherwise we wouldn't be able to understand them. But they are fundamentally different in activity.

As an astrologer and yogi, I have always told my students who teach and guide others, "When interacting with a dreamer, one must speak the language of dreams." Spiritual teachings and teachers embody an awakened, fully unified consciousness. Yet in order to reach those who are dreaming, they must still speak in the language of dreams.

In *Yoga Vasistha Sara*, Ramana Maharshi writes, "Just as fire born out of wind is extinguished by the same wind, so also that which is born of imagination is destroyed by imagination itself." Spiritual practices are based on concepts. No concepts are ultimately true. However, we can use one kind of concept to neutralize another kind of concept. Vasistha also states that we use one kind of matter (soap) to remove another kind of matter (soil). Or to think of it another way, we can use the sharp point of a thorn to remove the thorn that is stuck in our skin.

We use our spiritual concepts until we can go beyond all our concepts. What you might currently imagine enlightenment to be is not what it is. Your concept may serve to inspire you forward, but always remember, one day, even that concept will have to be released. Can you imagine living without any concepts? You don't have to. Continue on your awakening path and you will experience life without concepts firsthand. Always remember how real our dreams seem when we are dreaming them. Then contemplate how that might apply to your waking state.

Since you are reading this text, it is most likely that the path of Kriya Yoga Vichara is the spiritual language of your own dream that will finally wake you up. In this regard, we always remember not to denigrate, judge or find fault with another's path. If Kriya is the path for you, it is a solitary, silent and personal path. It requires no external validation, nor does it require comparison with anyone else's chosen path.

Your dreams do not affect the dreams of the person sleeping next to you. We all dream our own dreams and find our own way to wakefulness. When we finally wake up, we will see that enlightenment was nothing at all like what we thought and all dreams and dreamers are an individualized expression of a wholistic infinite and eternal consciousness in which all possibilities exist.

This is a final realization of advanced spiritual practice.

Chapter Three

GURU AND INITIATION

The guru is your own Self. As your consciousness becomes clearer and more internally radiant, you begin to see and experience directly that every thing, situation and circumstance is another facet of your eternal infinite Self. The guru, also existing as a concept in time and space, is not different.

When I was a child, I believed that there was a man named Santa Claus who brought presents to good little boys and girls on the holiday of Christmas. When I was eight to 12 years old, I believed that a man named Jesus was crucified for my sins. I felt that if I prayed to this long dead person that I would be assisted in my life's goals and that I might experience spiritual salvation. In my teenage years, I had come to the conclusion, what I secretly suspected, that this was not true. By the age of 13, I was exploring other religious and philosophical traditions, mostly pagan and occult, looking for something to feed my desire to know what was real and to know the true relationship between myself and the concept I had of divinity.

In my 19th year, I discovered *Autobiography of a Yogi* and the path of Kriya Yoga. I had already been introduced to the ideas of yoga, meditation and Self-realization through my previous self-directed studies, but it was this particular strain of spirituality that called to me most dearly. Not long after, I met a living student of Paramahansa Yogananda and was initiated into the path of Kriya Yoga. Over the next 12 years, I would go through the initiation ceremony at least once a year, and sometimes twice if I could. I would spend a few weeks a year on retreat and meet with my guru regularly.

During this time in my life, the guru was an embodied, living breathing person. He taught me the Kriya procedures and also the higher Kriya practices, which will also be covered in this text. He gave me some good advice, he gave me some bad advice, and he gave me some advice that didn't matter one way or another. Over this 12-year period, I learned eventually that he, like all embodied gurus, was actually a human being with a personality and his own opinions and quirks.

Throughout this 12-year process of discipleship, I came to an even greater realization about the guru. The guru is not limited to a single individual. Although, if our mind feels that is necessary, that will be our experience. The guru is in every breath and in every moment if we are consciously able to be aware of it. The guru can express through the voice of a child, through a passage in a book, through an uncomfortable experience, through a moment of silence or in any other manner necessary to quicken our inner work. This was a most liberating yet painful realization to have.

It is easy to release childish ideas, like Santa Claus is real or that a spiritual figure you've never met who died 2,000 years ago can really have any bearing on your current soul's incarnation. Yet, to realize that the one you revered and called guru, is really just a man after all, can shatter one's feelings of security on the spiritual path. It can be a difficult thing to accept, that your powerful spiritual experiences during initiation ceremonies were not the result of anyone other than your own intensive spiritual practice and receptivity. It is a strange thing to be forced to see that the only trust you need, is that trust in your Self. Yet, it is also part of the path and I feel quite necessary for those who believe their spiritual liberation is dependent on another being.

It was painful and it took a number of years to finally come to terms with this reality. Yet, it was liberating beyond words, as well. Before I nurtured the idea that I had to drive half a day to visit with someone who could "give" me spiritual experiences or a boost to my spiritual growth. Now it was simple and refreshing to sit quietly, no matter where I was, in my own home, or on a mountaintop, and experience that same transcendence, using the Kriya techniques. Before I felt I had to think of, honor and give energy to my guru lineage before I could experience the liberating results of Kriya practice. Now, all I had to do was acknowledge the infinite consciousness within and around me. No one else was necessary. It was this realization that led me to understand that the guru was not a single person but the wholeness of life existing in every moment. It was my very Self, and it has always been, and always will be accessible without need of an intermediary. There is no sense or use in continuing the idea that we cannot experience Self-realization right here and now so long as we have the proper intentions, healthy mind set and proper tools for the job.

I relate my experiences with guru not to deter you from learning from knowledgeable or skillful people but to help you see that your mind is powerful and what you believe about a person or circumstance might lead you to overlook something obvious — that the divine reality is ever present and requires only that you acknowledge it and follow the necessary steps to realize it. An authentic guru will not claim importance or require dependence. An authentic guru will not put on airs. He or she will share information, what works, and let you do the rest.

Although it was sometimes hard to take, my guru has always done this, even when I wasn't aware of it. And the relationship is clearer and stronger than ever because of it. The result was not greater dependence on a person or loss of Self in another's personality, but a greater clarity of the immediacy of the Self as the omniscient Seer.

I share this so you can begin to contemplate the possibility that all life is an aspect of your Self. Consider that the supreme intelligence, that has given structure to every cell of your body and being, created an environment for you in which you can breathe, work, love and experience all life, does not require an intermediary. By your own personal acknowledgement of this fact, you can experience it directly.

The Catholics admit we need a priest to connect with God. The Hindus say we need a guru. These are man-made beliefs. These beliefs serve you early in your spiritual development, *and they are necessary steps on the path*. The notion of Santa Claus helped me to behave and be a good boy as a child, but in time, that belief had to be resolved. If we wish to advance our spiritual realization, we must eventually take responsibility for our own inner work and quit placing the responsibility on others, even one's own divine embodied guru.

Of the advanced spiritual men and women I have known, this same sentiment has been shared. There is no reason for it to be otherwise. It is true, devotion to a guru, or to an aspect of divinity, can inspire us to feel peace and love. Yet at this stage in our development, it is important to choose to feel peace and love for the simple fact that we can, not because someone else requires it or inspires it. As liberated spiritual beings, it is our choice to experience love and divine communion. In fact, however we feel internally, is ultimately our choice.

I have learned important spiritual lessons from many people over the years. Some were people specifically playing the role of a spiritual teacher, some were family members, some were friends, and some were people I did not like. Twice a homeless person spoke to me directly and specifically to spiritual questions I was pondering. From each I learned something. From each was the guru speaking through the body of another person directly to my need. You may have experienced this, too, although you may not have been conscious of it.

I also learned from books, such as *Vasistha's Yoga*, *The Yoga Sutras of Patanjali* and *The Bhagavad Gita*. Within these texts, I found many answers to my questions and was led to profound contemplations. The guru can appear through many mediums, even books, but always it is only a reflection of your inner Self.

Rather than look outside of yourself, when you meditate, honor that divinity, that infinite Self within. Do not expect it to appear as a blinding light or a surge of ecstasy, although that may happen occasionally. Honor it as your simple heart beat, the rise and fall of your breath, the warmth within your being, or even the space within and around you.

When you are in nature, notice the breeze through the trees, the rain falling on your head, the sunshine over the field, the Moon reflected on the water, or the song of birds. Acknowledge and honor that sacred intelligence, which makes all these experiences possible. That is your very Self, and your eternal guru, from which you are never separate.

Then if you need counsel or coaching on your spiritual techniques or practices, find someone accomplished in these things. Ask for guidance and assistance. The guru will give it to you through them. This is how the guru appears in this era.

A WORD OF CAUTION

Be aware that it is important to be perceptive and observant in relationship to those whom we see as a teacher or guru. Do they actually embody a presence of peace and clarity? Do they engender doubt, fear or anxiety? Do they make you feel less than what you are? Do they acknowledge your innate pure infinite nature despite your actions or lifestyle choices? If you pay attention to how you feel around them or when you attune to them, you will get a sense of their inner consciousness.

Make sure those teachers you approach or learn from embody your spiritual goals internally. If they do not, it is best to avoid them. You must also learn to trust yourself in this matter. It is easy to be misled if you do not trust yourself or know how to see through external presentations. Remember, many of you are looking for a sense of security and completion, and there are plenty of crafty people who know this, and know how to capitalize on it. Just because someone claims to be a teacher, part of a lineage, to have divine realization, does not mean they do. A person may even be authentically of a respected tradition and still have no capacity for teaching in the truest sense.

I can only give general advice about recognizing a helpful teacher. The person may challenge your beliefs without disrespecting them. The teachings shared when applied as instructed will clarify and make peaceful your consciousness. Every day, in the practice of those teachings, will give you greater capacity to appreciate the beauty and wholeness of life all around you, even during times of trial.

KRIYA YOGA INITIATION

An initiation is a new beginning. It is an event or circumstance where you consciously decide to step into a new way of being. Spiritual initiations may be spontaneous or they may manifest as a well-planned ritual or ceremony. Whether spontaneous or planned, it is not the external event that empowers the process, it is inner shift of consciousness that the outer activity represents. It is the individual's capacity to maintain that shift of consciousness that will ultimately reflect the value or impact of initiation.

I have seen hundreds of people go through spiritual initiation ceremonies. I have performed many Kriya initiations myself since being authorized to do so in 2005. It was often a mystery to me why some people would have profound and lasting changes, spiritually speaking, due to an initiation ceremony while others did not seem to change or experience any kind of elevation of consciousness at all.

Because of this, I remained observant and curious over the years. I began to see a pattern. People who benefited most from the initiation process possessed certain attitudes. First, they took the initiation process seriously. Second, they did not expect it to change them overnight. Third, they knew the initiation represented a new beginning, and it was up to them to continue consciously affirming a new way of being in the world.

A serious student of Kriya Yoga does not approach initiation with doubt or whimsical curiosity. A Kriya Yogi knows internally that it is the correct step in their spiritual path. There is no doubt.

Many people ask, "Am I ready to be initiated?" or "Do you think it will help me to be initiated?" These questions indicate doubt. There is nothing wrong with doubt, but I would say, if you have it, then do not concern your self with initiation. However, if you have learned about Kriya Yoga and you feel with utmost certainty it is your path, and initiation is the right thing to do, then find a way to make it happen.

You will then take it seriously. You will approach the process with reverence, humility and a willingness to learn. Your sincerity will empower the process. Otherwise, you will be initiated, hoping that it's going to help you in some nebulous way. When you find out the initiation process was just a beginning, possessing no innate magic of its own to change your life, you will give up, move on, and look for the next magic key to your salvation.

Committing to a spiritual path, any spiritual path, will always have some kind of initiation. This can be an obvious ritual or ceremony, a spontaneous experience, or coming to a firm decision all on your own. These are all initiations. They are all beginnings, the first step on a fulfilling journey. It is a journey that will challenge your very concepts of divinity and reality. It may bring ecstasy and joy. It may also bring tedious routine or require some painful changes that you do not want to make. Initiation is the beginning of the journey, a journey that may take years, decades or lifetimes to complete. The time it takes is not important. It is the fact you are committed to walking it, no matter where it leads, that is important.

Those who have a spontaneous spiritual experience, or a wonderful initiation experience and think that is all there is, have not grasped the immensity of what it means to explore an infinite consciousness. This is why, in our current era, there are so many people talking about spirituality and non-duality, acting like teachers, with nothing worthwhile to offer. They had an experience, but did not use that boost of insight to propel them onto the long path of Self-realization.

I often see initiation as a new spiritual start. What you do with that start will have a profound say on how it actually affects your spiritual realizations. Imagine that you have been living beyond your means. You have gotten yourself into great debt. You finally realize what you have been doing is wrong, and so you turn to a benefactor for help. If you are sincere, maybe the benefactor will pay off your debts and give you a large sum of money to rebuild your life. Now imagine you are cautious, careful and committed. You learn how to take that money and make it work for you, and you build a resourceful life. That is what happens when initiated. Your debts are spiritually paid and you are given a small gift to get you started on your own work.

Imagine the opposite. Imagine you are in debt and you have no motivation to get out of debt or to stop doing what is putting you in debt. You go to a benefactor and he pays your debts and gives you a gift to start anew. Yet again, you waste it and return to your old ways. You have wasted the opportunity. You can continue returning to the benefactor, and he may, with hope in his heart, continue to assist you. But in time, he will see that you are not sincere and do not have the capacity to appreciate or benefit from his help. This is why seeking out initiations or new and different paths ultimately never works. It requires you actually have the honesty and sincerity to make the most of what you will be given.

Initiation is a new start. What you make of it is up to you.

THE MECHANICS OF KRIYA INITIATION

The mechanics of an official Kriya Yoga Initiation include the following. First, the prepared student brings a fruit, a flower and a monetary donation to the teacher at the appointed time. The teacher instructs the student on the proper methods to perform the chosen Kriya techniques. The first techniques usually taught are a life force arousal technique, Kriya pranayama and a method of internalization of attention (pratyahara) called Jyoti Mudra. Other techniques may be taught later, after the student has sufficient skill with the techniques mentioned above. The teacher and student meditate together and perform the Kriya practices together. A blessing may be shared, and the student goes on his or her way, ready to practice daily.

The fruit represents the student's renunciation of the fruits of their karma. The flower represents the devotion and commitment they offer to the path. The monetary donation represents the student's willingness to dedicate their time, energy and resources to support their chosen path.

This is no different than any other commitment. Those who want to be successful musicians must give up any distractions that pull them away from their art. They must maintain a sense of devotion and commitment to a practice and educational schedule. They must be willing to pay for instruments, tutoring or anything else that will support them along the way. Greatness in any endeavor requires the same commitment, sacrifice and devotion.

As mentioned previously, it is not wise to deify a teacher. Yet it is wise to learn from someone skillful and accomplished in your chosen goal. Only one who has practiced and refined their own path can accurately teach the techniques and help you avoid mistakes they have made, thereby quickening your progress.

In many traditions, teaching is not simply mechanical. Imagine that a person has an energetic imprint for success. If you spend time with that person, you may begin to energetically adopt that same imprint. This makes it easier for you to experience what they experience. This can be true in martial arts, in musical accomplishment, financial understanding, health, and even in regards to spiritual realization. Typically, we become like those with whom we associate.

You can see this in a more obvious way by paying attention to how you feel around someone who is angry, sad, anxious, joyful or peaceful. If you are willing and receptive, you can easily move into the same state.

An accomplished spiritual master will maintain that state of peace and clarity. They are not trying to affect you, yet if you want to attune to that, you can. In this way, they are not doing the work for you, but giving you a glimpse of a possibility. By modeling your behavior after theirs or asking what they did to attain that, you can now begin the work to shape your consciousness in the same way.

During a Kriya initiation ceremony, the teacher will do his or her best to fully embody this state of clarity. Through the blessing process, the intention is to share that clarity with the student. This is then built up during one's own private Kriya practice sessions.

Chapter Four

KRIYA MEDITATION TECHNIQUES

The following description of meditation and the basic practices have been reprinted from my previous book *Kriya Yoga: Continuing the Lineage of Enlightenment*. Before undertaking the practices given during initiation, meditate using the basic procedures given below for at least six months. Once you are proficient in mantra, chanting through the chakras, inner light and sound contemplation, and sushumna breathing, you will be prepared to begin the specific Kriya techniques. Also, be sure to read this entire chapter before exploring the techniques described.

BASIC MEDITATION PROCEDURES

Meditation clears the mind of conditionings and elevates awareness above the influence of samskaras (mental impressions with the potential to influence experiences). Samskaras are like impurities in glass. The more impurities in our consciousness, the harder it is to understand the world and our relationship to it correctly. Kriya Yoga practice is concerned with understanding higher realities to the same degree that it is concerned with living effectively in our current incarnation. When meditation is practiced intelligently, we gain understanding of higher realities *and* can relate better to the situations around us. We know our spiritual growth is authentic when we are internally peaceful while also experiencing greater harmony and effectiveness in our day-to-day experiences.

When practiced with attention, the following meditation techniques are helpful in eliciting superconsciousness. These specific techniques can be used by anyone, yet are considered to be valuable preliminary practices for those aspiring to learn the higher Kriya pranayamas, given during initiation.

Beginning meditators are advised to sit for 20 minutes once or twice a day. Proficient meditators can sit for 45 minutes or longer, as long as the practice is alert and attentive. Passive daydreaming, slipping into subconscious states, or sleeping are not useful.

Set aside the same time each day for meditation practice so that it becomes part of your regular routine. Dedicating a place in the house or a special chair for meditation practice is also useful. It may help to have a ritual, such as lighting a candle or saying a prayer.

Consistently practice the techniques until you can be superconscious. We know we are superconscious when we are no longer unduly disturbed by thoughts or distractions. We can sit quietly and calmly, yet alert and awake, when in a superconscious state.

Basic Mantra Meditation

Sitting up straight and comfortable, bring your awareness to your breathing. Take a deep breath and exhale, letting your body relax while keeping your head and neck erect. Then let the breath flow in and out naturally. Do not force the breathing. Simply observe it.

Once settled and focused on the breath, introduce the mantra "so hum." Mentally chant the mantra. Hear the sound "so" resonating within your field of awareness on the inhale.

Mentally listen to the sound "hum" resonating within your field of awareness on the exhale. To fully engage your attention in this process, imagine each syllable vibrating within your being.

Let your awareness be drawn further inward on each inhalation and exhalation. In time, thoughts and emotions will settle and you will experience inner peace. When this occurs, ignore the mantra. Sit in the peace generated by practice. If thoughts, memories or emotions emerge, repeat the technique to reestablish your inner poise.

Inner Light and Sound Contemplation

In Vedic teachings, Om is considered the primordial vibration that emanates from the source of creation. Meditate on Om to restore your awareness to its original pure wholeness. Om can be chanted audibly or mentally. It can also be contemplated by gazing into the spiritual eye and listening to subtle sound frequencies around the head.

In a quiet place with little external light, assume a meditation posture. Take a few deep breaths, relaxing your body on each exhale.

Once settled, bring your attention up to the higher brain centers. Be aware of the space between your eyebrows and the crown of the head.

With your eyes closed, gaze into the darkness of your closed eyelids. Imagine the darkness has depth and space. Lift your gaze slightly upward as if looking at the top of a distant mountain. Continue to gaze off through the dark inner space of your closed eyes.

Now, listen for an inner sound current within your ear. It may sound like a high-pitched hum, a ringing, or another constant tone. Examine this sound. Listen for any change in the sound. Listen behind the sound. Do you hear another sound behind it? Does the one you are listening to get louder? Continue to follow the sounds as they change and draw you deeper into meditation.

With practice, the electrical activity of the nervous system you are listening to will enable you to hear the Om vibration. Allow your small sense of Self to dissolve into the sounds you perceive.

As you practice this technique, while keeping your attention in the higher brain centers and looking inward, you may also begin to see lights or geometrical patterns in your spiritual eye. When this occurs, let them attract your attention. Contemplating inner light may enable you to more easily hear the Om vibration. As you go deeper into the sound current, look through the inner light. Feel that you are piercing the light, as if you are moving through your forehead into the source of the light.

Just as the initial sounds you hear around your head are the electrical activity of the nervous system, initial light perceptions are the result of brain activity. To practice inner light and sound contemplation, you may want to practice the basic mantra technique first. The calmer and more internalized you are, the easier it will be.

Chanting Through the Chakras

Sit upright in a meditation posture. Bring your attention to the base of your spine, your first chakra. Maintain your attention there for five to ten breaths. Bring your attention up to the second chakra. Rest there for a few moments.

Continue bringing your attention up through the chakras to the crown chakra. As you go up through the chakras, mentally chant the appropriate mantra at each chakra.

Chakra	Location	Mantric Syllable
Root	Base of the spine	Lum
Sacrum	Small of the back	Vum
Navel	Behind the navel	Rum
Heart	Between the shoulder blades	Yum
Throat	Back of the neck	Hum
Third Eye	Between the eyebrows	Om
Crown	Higher brain	Bum

Then go down to the base of your spine chanting the mantra at each chakra. Repeat the procedure two or three times. Conclude your practice at the crown chakra.

Sushumna Breathing

To practice sushumna breathing, meditate as you normally do. When the mind is calm and emotions settled, put your attention in your spine. Feel your spine, from the base to the crown chakra. Imagine a hollow tube within the spine.

Breathe slightly deeper than normal and in a relaxed manner. As you inhale, use a gentle act of will to pull your life force up through the hollow tube in your spine. If you do not feel a sensation of prana ascending through the spine, imagine what it would feel like. When the inhalation is complete, the pranic current will be in the crown chakra. Hold your breath for a second, and then exhale easily and without force while noting the descending flow of the current. Let the breath exhale of its own accord. Do not force the breath out. Let the energetic current flow back down your spine like water.

When silence prevails in your awareness and you are absorbed in existence-being, pull the current up to the top of the head one last time. Let your breathing occur naturally. Keep the current and your attention in the crown chakra. Sit in the silence until you conclude your meditation practice.

INITIAL KRIYA YOGA PROCEDURES

The following techniques are taught during Kriya Initiation. They are for meditation practitioners who are devoted to the path of Kriya as it has been handed down from teacher to student, in one form or another, over the centuries. I encourage you to not rush into practicing these techniques until you feel comfortable and proficient with the meditation procedures already provided above. Patience and the capacity to take an honest Self-inventory of your current state of preparedness is a quality of every authentic Kriya Yogi.

When you are ready for the practices described below, first read the description thoroughly and repeatedly. Make sure you understand what is being stated. Then gently practice each technique. Do not do it mechanically, but give your full attention to each step in the process. Practice and experimentation will be your best teacher. If necessary, ask a yoga teacher who is familiar with the following practices to assist your understanding and application.

In the next chapter, we will explore how to successfully create a Kriya routine for your skill level.

Life Force Arousal Technique

The life force arousal technique is practiced at the beginning of each Kriya meditation session. There are two variations of this technique. If you are a regular Hatha Yoga practitioner, you may enjoy the Maha Mudra procedure. If you have difficulty with flexibility, or cannot practice the Maha Mudra for various reasons, you may use the simpler procedure. Both are effective. If you do decide to use the Maha Mudra technique, ask a yoga teacher to help you perfect the postures and movement.

The purpose of these life force arousal techniques is to gently activate the pranic energy in your lower chakras. They act to prepare the astral body for more intensive Kriya Pranayama.

Maha Mudra Life Force Arousal Procedure

Step 1: Sit on the floor and extend both legs straight out in front of you. Keep a straight yet comfortable upright position (as in Dandasana Hatha Yoga posture).

Step 2: Bend your left leg, so that you can sit on the heel of your left foot. Your back is still upright. Your right leg is still extended directly in front of you. The heel of your left foot is now situated so that you are sitting on the heel, and the heel is directly under your perineum.

Step 3: Bend your right leg, so that you can pull the knee towards your chest. Use both hands to hold the shin and pull the knee towards the chest. The right foot will be flat on the ground in front of you.

Step 4: Take a deep easy breath. Exhale. Relax.

Step 5: Gently tighten the muscles in area of the perineum. This will feel like you are gently tensing the anal sphincter and the genital area. Simultaneously suck in your belly as though you were pulling your abdominal muscles inward and upward.

Step 6: Inhale and using the Sushumna breathing practice, imagine or feel that you are pulling life force up from the base of the spine through the spine, through the neck, up to the crown of the head and then, following the curve of the skull, imagine the life force flowing to the spiritual eye center. Hold the breath momentarily.

Step 7: Lower your chin down to your chest, gently tensing the muscles around the throat. Lower the right leg straight in front of you.

Step 8: Bend forward and reach for your extended foot with both hands. Grasp the foot or the calf (whichever is most comfortable) and gently pull your torso forward to gently stretch the spine. At this point, you are still holding your breath.

Step 9: Let go of your foot or leg. Lift your torso back upright. Lift your chin. Relax the throat and the perineum area. Exhale. Imagine or feel the life force flowing back down the spine gently.

Step 10: Repeat Steps two to nine with the opposite leg.

Step 11: Extend both legs out in front of your body (as in Dandasana Hatha Yoga posture). Then repeat Steps four to nine with both legs extended.

Then sit in your regular meditation posture for the duration of your session.

Simplified Life Force Arousal Procedure

Step 1: Sit in your regular meditation posture. Bring your awareness to the spiritual eye center. Inhale gently and deeply. Relax on the exhale.

Step 2: : Gently tighten the muscles in area of the perineum. This will feel like you are gently tensing the anal sphincter and the genital area. Simultaneously suck in your belly as though you were pulling your abdominal muscles inward and upward.

Step 3: Inhale and using the Sushumna breathing practice, imagine or feel that you are pulling life force up from the base of the spine through the spine to the level opposite the navel, ***the third chakra area only***. Hold the breath.

Step 4: Lower your chin down to your chest, gently tensing the muscles around the throat. Hold the breath for a moment longer while keeping your attention on the prana that has ascended up from the base of the spine to the third chakra level behind the navel.

Step 5: Relax the throat and the perineum area as you lift your head back to an upright position. As you relax, exhale and imagine or feel the life force descending back down the spine.

Step 6: Repeat this process three to four times.

Step 7: After the final repetition, sit quietly for a few minutes before proceeding to Kriya Pranayama.

The purpose of these procedures is to encourage awareness of the life force as it circulates through the spine. It also enables us to be more aware of the spine in general, which is essential for proper Kriya practice.

Kriya Pranayama

Kriya Pranayama is an intensive method of Sushumna breathing. It will utilize the same method of drawing pranic life force up through the center of the spine on the inhalation and feeling the life force current descend during exhalation. Kriya Pranayama is practiced after the life force arousal technique.

Step 1: Assume your comfortable upright meditation posture. Bring your awareness to your spiritual eye center (the space between the eyebrows), the brain and spine. Simply be aware of these areas of your body.

With your eyes closed, rest your attention at your spiritual eye center by gazing forward and upward through the darkness of your eyelids. Direct your gaze slightly upward, as if you were looking at the point where the ceiling and wall comes together at the far end of a room. Do not strain your gaze by trying to look directly upward. Imagine you are gazing through the darkness of your closed eyes *through* the spiritual eye center.

Step 2: Take a deep easy breath. Exhale and relax.

Step 3: Open your mouth about one centimeter, just enough so air can flow in through your mouth while you breathe. Inhale slowly, deeply and gently. As the air flows in through the mouth, gently tense the throat until you feel the air striking the back of the throat, giving a cool sensation. If you practice

Hatha Yoga, this will be similar to ujjayi breathing, but with the mouth slightly open.

Note: When you breathe normally, you cannot hear the sound of your breath flowing through your throat. When gently constricting the throat, as described here, you will be able to hear the gentle rush of air as it flows through your throat. This need not be excessive, so that everyone around you would hear it, but just enough that you can hear it as you practice.

Step 4: The open mouth and gently tensed throat will create a cool sensation on the back of the throat as you inhale. Associate that cool sensation with the life force ascending up through the spine. As you inhale in this manner, imagine or feel the life force being pulled up from the base of the spine, through the spine, through the brain, to the crown of the head and then over the forehead to the spiritual eye center between the eyebrows. Pause briefly, holding your awareness on this cool sensation that has ascended up through the spine, with the breath.

Step 5: Relax the throat. Allow the body to exhale. You are not forcing the exhale. You simply let the lungs empty their air. As you exhale, imagine or feel a warm soothing life force current flowing down from the brain through the spine, to the base of the spine. Pause briefly, holding your awareness on this warm soothing sensation that has descended down through the spine.

Step 6: Repeat this process 14 times, if you are a new Kriya practitioner. Proficient practitioners can increase this number as described below.

Step 7: On the last repetition, inhale, pull the cool current up through the spine to the crown of the head. Hold your awareness at the crown, maintaining attention on the life force that has been drawn to the crown. When you exhale, keep your awareness at the crown. Let the body breathe normally, while your attention is still gently resting at the crown. You no longer need to pay attention to the breath, only the crown of your head. Sit in the silence, the poise-after-effects-tranquility generated by the practice.

Beginners are advised to practice Kriya Pranayama 14 times once a day or twice a day, if you are able to schedule two meditation sessions.

After six months to one year of such practice, one can then increase the repetitions to 24 times. This is done over a period of days. After you are ready to increase your Kriya Pranayamas, you do so by adding one pranayama a day until you reach 24. On day one, you do 15 pranayamas. On day two, you do 16. On day three, you do 17. Continue in this way until you reach 24. Then continue practicing 24 repetitions a day from then on. Every six months to one year, you can increase your number of Kriya Pranayamas by 12 in the same manner. Year one, practice 14. Year two, practice 24. Year three, practice 36. Year four, practice 48, and so on.

Please note that the number of repetitions is not as important as the quality. This process does not work better if you do 108 repetitions mechanically, rather than doing 24 with intention and feeling. Do not aim for high numbers of pranayama, aim for depth of practice and quality of feeling as you practice.

Do keep the breath slow and even throughout practice. You want to make sure you are always getting enough oxygen, so do not force yourself to breathe slower than you can, but do endeavor to make the breath deeper and longer than your average breathing.

Only beginners are advised to breathe through the mouth. This helps one to begin to feel the upward flow of cool electrical current during practice. With practice and attention, you will begin to feel the cool ascension of the life force up through the spine, and the warm soothing flow as it descends on the exhale. When this occurs, you may then breathe through your nose instead of the mouth.

There are a few variations on this technique of which I am aware. The above-described method is what was taught to me during initiation. Do not worry about variations on this technique. It is the simple practice of intentionally pulling the life force up through the spine and letting it descend that is important. Of equal importance is holding the attention at the crown or spiritual eye center, while remaining as the witnessing presence in the after-effects-poise-tranquility of the practice.

I once heard that Yogananda said that by practicing Kriya but not remaining after the practice, sitting in the silence, is like preparing a gourmet meal and instead of eating it, throwing it all away after preparation was complete. This is a hint at how important it is to remain in the silence *after* practicing the techniques.

Be sure to pay attention to the clarity generated after the practice. As you go about your day, after meditation, remember that clarity and peace. Imagine what it would be like if every moment was imbued with that same clear presence. With practice, you will learn to be superconscious whether you are meditating or not. This is also Kriya practice.

When Not To Practice Kriya Pranayama Techniques

The body is animated and organized by numerous currents of life force energy. For example, some pranas in the body stimulate digestion and assimilation. Others are at work in elimination. Still others deal with promoting proper circulation and heat within the body. Kriya practices are dynamic life force activating and purifying techniques, and because of this, they need to be practiced with care.

So long as the body and mind are relatively healthy, we can practice Kriya. The times to avoid practicing Kriya are when the body or mind are unwell. Avoid practicing the Kriya techniques, which circulate life force through the spine, when you are fatigued, physically ill, emotionally or psychologically disturbed. Women should avoid practicing during their time of menstruation or when pregnant. People with psychiatric problems that make them prone to hallucinations, fantasy, delusions or other mental distortions should also avoid the life force circulating practices.

Mantra meditation, chanting through the chakras and simple breath awareness can be practiced at times when Kriya life force circulation techniques are not advised.

Jyoti Mudra

Jyoti Mudra is known as Yoni Mudra, as well as the inner light technique. Jyoti means light. Yoni is a reference to the birth canal through which we are born. This technique usually gives one a sense of seeing light in the spiritual eye as if passing through a long tunnel, similar to the birth canal. It enables us to see and merge with the inner light of consciousness. It is practiced last, because we can usually more readily see the inner light during meditation when our mind and consciousness is alert, aware and conscious, yet also relaxed and poised. It is the third procedure in the complete Kriya practice.

After you have practiced the life force arousal technique, and completed your Kriya Pranayama, then practice Jyoti Mudra:

Step 1: Take your hands and cover your eyes. The tips of your fingers should be just above your eyebrows. The tips of your third and fourth fingers will probably touch each other. Your palms will gently rest on your cheekbones. Your thumbs cover the holes of your ears. This will block out more external light from your closed eyes. It will also block out any sounds in the environment.

Step 2: Inhale. Exhale and relax.

Step 3: Inhale in the same fashion as you did when practicing the Kriya Pranayama, as in Steps 3 and 4 above.

Step 4: Holding your breath and keeping your awareness at the spiritual eye center, again look out and slightly upward through the darkness of your closed eyes. Imagine the darkness of your closed eyes has depth and space, so as you look through that darkness, you imagine you are looking out *through* it.

Step 5: Still holding your breath, mentally chant Om, Om, Om, Om, Om, Om, etc. Imagine that with each chant of the syllable Om, you are moving through or piercing that darkness. Continue chanting Om, moving through the spiritual eye with each repetition for as long as you can comfortably hold your breath.

Step 6: When you feel you need to breathe again, stop chanting. Exhale gently, imagine or feel the life force descending down through the spine with the breath. Keep your hands in position. Sit quietly until your breathing has returned to normal.

Step 7: Repeat this process three to five times. On the last time, instead of stopping chanting and allowing the current to descend when you exhale, hold attention at the spiritual eye. Keep your hands in position. Continue chanting Om repeatedly, and continue imagining or feeling you are piercing or moving through the darkness of your closed eyelids. At this point, you have exhaled, you are still gazing through the spiritual eye and chanting Om, your hands are still in position, but you have disregarded the breath and allowed your breathing to return to normal.

Step 8: Eventually, if you get tired of holding your arms up to cover your eyes and ears, remove your hands from your face and let your hands rest on your thighs. Continue holding awareness at the spiritual eye center. Conclude the internal chanting of Om, and simply sit in the silence. Watching.
Enjoy the after-effects-tranquility of the practice.

During this practice, you may see brilliant light within the spiritual eye. You may experience an expansion of conscious awareness. You may experience surges of peace or bliss. You also may see nothing at all. You may only experience the sound of your inner thoughts chanting Om and the darkness behind your eyes. We are all different in our temperaments and how meditation affects our perceptions.

If you see light, or have other pleasant experiences, welcome them and then let them go. Imagine that as you chant, you are flowing through those perceptions, piercing them and moving more fully into pure consciousness. Do not become attached to any meditation experience. It is fine to enjoy experiences, but clinging to any experience, even a meditative experience, can delay the revelation of our Self-realization.

Remember that some inner perceptions are produced by the brain or other physiological stimulus. Sometimes people accidentally push on their eyeballs while resting their hands on their face during Jyoti Mudra. This can also produce lights in the eyes. Do not do this. It is bad for your eyes, and it is not a meditative perception.

You will know when you see the inner light and it is not a physiological perception. It will look as real as the sun does in the sky, and be even more brilliant without being blinding. As mentioned previously, this is only seen when the meditator has trained the body and mind to experience deep relaxation, without losing consciousness, while remaining aware. This takes practice. Once mastered, one can learn to see the inner light at will and meditate on that radiance.

More will be said on specific beginner, intermediate and advanced Kriya practices and routines in the next chapter. For now, it is important to know that the sequence begins with the life force arousal technique. Then Kriya Pranayama is practiced. Then Jyoti Mudra.

2nd, 3rd and 4th Kriya Initiation Procedures

After several years of the above practices, one may be inclined to include the following advanced techniques. These advanced techniques were given to me by my teacher five years after I had been practicing daily the Kriya procedures mentioned above.

I do not use these advanced procedures often. I have found that the simplicity of the life force arousal technique, Kriya Pranayama and Jyoti Mudra are more than enough to elicit superconsciousness and lead into profound contemplation. I utilize these advanced techniques specifically when I am sitting in meditation for longer than two or three hours, or if I am doing a private retreat where I have the capacity to sit and meditate in silence more often than my usual schedule.

Due to the complexity of these techniques, I do feel it is useful to learn them directly from someone already proficient with them. However, I am including their description in this work for the sake of completeness. Personally, I do not teach these to meditators until I have seen that they are fully dedicated to their practice and have been consistent with their Kriya practice for at least three years.

Put your focus on the three Kriya procedures mentioned previously. If after three to five years you want to begin experimenting with the advanced techniques, do so at your discretion. Remember, if you are not able to experience a superconscious state through the combination of life force arousal technique, Kriya Pranayama and Jyoti Mudra, you need to refine those practices first. The advanced techniques will only work after you have developed a good foundation in eliciting superconsciousness through Kriya Pranayama.

Second Tier Kriya Practice

Variation #1

This first variation is almost exactly the same as the *Chanting Through The Chakras* procedure mentioned earlier. The only difference is you do not chant the seed syllables, such as "lum," "vum," "rum," "yum," "hum," "Om" and "bum." Instead, you only chant Om at each chakra.

When you begin this practice, first put your attention in your spine and hold your awareness at the spiritual eye center simultaneously. Then imagine that you can feel Om pulsing and vibrating in each chakra, as you chant through the chakra. For example, when you are chanting Om at the first chakra, imagine you can feel Om pulsing and vibrating through that chakra with each mental repetition of Om. Do this with each chakra for the duration of the practice. If any distractions arise while you are chanting, imagine that every time you feel Om vibrate within the chakra you are focused on, that the distraction dissolves or disintegrates. Then return your awareness back to the procedure.

This variation is good to keep you engaged in the process of meditation during longer sessions. It is also advised for people who cannot or are not able to practice the regular Kriya Pranayama for whatever reason. It is a potent substitute for Kriya Pranayama if practiced with intention and attention.

Variation #2

This variation I learned from a Kriya Yoga teacher of a different lineage than my own. I have found it very useful and often do practice this in place of the standard Kriya Pranayama.

Essentially, you practice Kriya Pranayama and add the first six seed syllables. As you inhale and pull the current of life force up through spine, you chant the appropriate seed syllable at the appropriate chakra. It does take practice to time the breath appropriately.

As you inhale, you start with your awareness at the base chakra and chant "lum." Continue the inhale and pulling the current up to the second chakra and chant "vum." Continue the inhale and pulling the current up to the third chakra and chant "rum." Continue the inhale and pulling the current up to the fourth chakra and chant "yum." Continue the inhale and pulling the current up to the fifth chakra and chant "hum." Continue the inhale and pulling the current up to the sixth chakra and chant "Om."

This is all done in one breath. You only chant the seed syllable once at each chakra. Once you have pulled the current up through the spine to the sixth chakra, you pause for a second or two. You then let the current descend naturally, and chant the seed syllables at the appropriate chakra in reverse order back down the spine. Pause for a second or two and repeat.

On the final repetition, as with Kriya Pranayama, inhale and pull the life force current all the way to the crown of the head. Keep your attention at the crown. Disregard the breath. Let the body exhale and then let the breath happen naturally. Rest in the silence with your attention at the crown chakra. Holding awareness at the crown attunes you to infinite-intelligence-bliss of your purest being. Sit with your awareness at the crown until you feel inclined to conclude your practice, or you need to refresh your practice by using another meditation technique.

This variation is done in place of the first Kriya Pranayama. Or it can be done later in a meditation session after practicing the first three Kriya procedures of life force arousal, Kriya Pranayama and Jyoti Mudra. If done after Jyoti Mudra, wait until you have sat in the silence for an extended duration and then practice variation #2 for 10 to 12 repetitions to refresh the meditation and enliven and relax the nervous system. You can, of course, increase the number of repetitions over time, making sure to stay in your comfort level.

Third Tier Kriya Practice

In this tier, we use the mantra "Om Namo Bhagavate Vasudevaya." Memorize the mantra. Research the proper pronunciation of the mantra, or ask someone proficient in mantra to help you pronounce the mantra correctly. Chant it aloud before meditation until you have it memorized and feel comfortable with the pronunciation.

After sitting for an extended duration in the silence after Jyoti Mudra, practice Kriya Pranayama again with this variation. Mentally chant the following syllables at each chakra as you pull the cool current up through the spine to the sixth chakra.

1st Chakra – Om
2nd Chakra – Naw
3rd Chakra – Mo
4th Chakra – Bhaw
5th Chakra – Gaw
6th Chakra – Vaw

Then pause for a second or two with your attention at the sixth chakra.

Gently, let your head roll slightly forward (chin moving towards the chest less than an inch) and then let the head roll or drop gently towards the left shoulder. At the same instant be aware of the 6th chakra and mentally say the syllable "Tey."

Then gently let your head roll slightly forward (chin moving towards the chest less than an inch) and then let the head roll or drop gently towards the right shoulder. At the same instant be aware of the 5th chakra and mentally say the syllable "Vaw."

Gently let your head roll or drop forward so the chin moves fully towards the chest. (Do not force the chin to the chest, just let the head drop chin to chest.) At the same instant be aware of the 4th chakra and mentally say the syllable "Su."

Lift the head, exhale, let the breath flow out naturally. As you imagine or feel the warm life force current descending down through the spine, mentally chant the following syllables at each chakra.

3rd Chakra – Dey
2nd Chakra – Vaw
1st Chakra – Yaw

Essentially, you are practicing Kriya Pranayama and chanting at each chakra as the current ascends and descends. On the inhale, you will be chanting this part of the mantra, "Om Namo bhagava..." While holding the breath and performing the head rolls, you will be chanting, "...te Vasu..." And on the exhale you will be chanting, "...devaya." As the life force ascends and descends, your awareness will briefly rest at each chakra as you chant the appropriate syllable of the mantra.

This process can be repeated three to four times. To conclude, practice Kriya Pranayama and pull the life force current all the way to the crown. Keep your attention at the crown. Disregard the breath. Let the body exhale and then let the breath happen naturally. Rest in the silence with your attention at the crown chakra. Sit with your awareness at the crown until you feel inclined to conclude your practice.

Fourth Tier Kriya Practice

After one year of consistent application of the Third Tier Kriya Practice, you may proceed to this stage.

The Fourth Tier is a variation of Tier Three. You practice it exactly the same, except you repeat the movement of the head from left, to right, to the chin to chest, three times before letting the current descend down through the spine and chanting "devaya" at the lower three chakras.

After sitting for an extended duration in the silence after Jyoti Mudra, practice Kriya Pranayama again with this variation.

Step 1: Mentally chant the following syllables at each chakra as you pull the cool current up through the spine to the sixth chakra.

1st Chakra – Om
2nd Chakra – Naw
3rd Chakra – Mo
4th Chakra – Bhaw
5th Chakra – Gaw
6th Chakra – Vaw

Step 2: Then pause for a second or two with your attention at the sixth chakra. Your breath is held.

Step 3: Gently let your head roll slightly forward (chin moving towards the chest less than an inch) and then let the head roll or drop gently towards the left shoulder. At the same instant be aware of the 6th chakra and mentally say the syllable "Tey."

Then gently let your head roll slightly forward (chin moving towards the chest less than an inch) and then let the head roll or drop gently towards the right shoulder. At the same instant be aware of the 5th chakra and mentally say the syllable "Vaw."

Gently let your head roll or drop forward so the chin moves fully towards the chest. (Do not force the chin to the chest, just let the head drop chin to chest.) At the same instant be aware of the 4th chakra and mentally say the syllable "Su."

Step 4: Lift the head. Continue to hold the breath.

Step 5: Repeat Steps 3 and 4 two more times.

Step 6: Exhale. Lift your head to a normal upright position. Let the breath flow out naturally. As you imagine or feel the warm life force current descending down through the spine, mentally chant the following syllables at each chakra.

3rd Chakra – Dey
2nd Chakra – Vaw
1st Chakra – Yaw

To conclude, practice Kriya Pranayama and pull the life force current all the way to the crown. Keep your attention at the crown. Disregard the breath. Let the body exhale and then let the breath happen naturally. Rest in the silence with your attention at the crown chakra. Sit with your awareness at the crown until you feel inclined to conclude your practice.

As you progress with this practice, you can increase the number of head rotations to your comfort level. Remember, never force yourself to hold your breath. Only hold the breath as long as is comfortable.

With all Kriya practices, quality of practice is better than quantity. Once you experience superconsciousness and internal peace, you can stop the mechanical technique and rest in the silent intelligent-knowing-bliss generated by the practice.

Chapter Five

ADDITIONAL CONSIDERATIONS

Meditation Gaze

During all meditation practices, the gaze of the eyes should be slightly upward. The best way to understand this is by imagining you are sitting in one corner of an average-sized room. While you are sitting in this room, you are looking up at the corner opposite you at the junction where the ceiling meets the walls. When you imagine this, notice that your eyes are not strained upward, looking straight up into your skull. The eyes are gently lifted, gazing out and upward at a slight angle.

When your eyes are closed and you gaze in this way, you will be gazing through the spiritual eye center. This is the best focal point for the gaze during meditation. It helps keep you alert, aware and energized. It prevents passive daydreaming and falling asleep. When practiced regularly during meditation, it gives command over your mental and emotional states, and with long-term practice can even give control over unconscious aspects of the body.

Tongue Position

The tongue can be placed so the tip of the tongue touches the roof of the mouth. Ideally, it should touch the junction between the bones in the roof of the mouth and the soft palate. This helps to complete the energetic circuit through which life force flows. Practitioners may notice this makes their Kriya practice more effective. Experimentation will be your best guide.

Some people recommend extreme practices such as severing the frenulum of the tongue, so the tongue can be directed into the nasal cavity above the throat. This is not necessary, nor is it advised. Our bodies are perfectly built for these Kriya practices. Anything that requires you to maim or injure your body is not necessary.

Meditation Seat

One's meditation seat should be firm yet comfortable. The meditation posture needs to be such, so that the back is straight and the head and neck are erect. I like to imagine that there is a string at the crown of my head lightly lifting the crown and aligning my head, back and neck. Whether you cross your legs or sit in a chair, what ultimately matters is that your back, neck and head are upright.

If you can sit comfortably in a cross-legged posture, such as Lotus Pose, or some variation, that is fine. However, it is not necessary.

You can meditate equally well in a chair with good back support and your feet flat on the floor in front of you. In fact, this is probably better for most people.

The goal of your meditation posture is to support you in your practice and provide as little distractions as possible so you can practice pratyahara effectively and internalize your attention. Your enlightenment will not come quicker if you force yourself into a cross-legged posture for two hours and injure your knees and your back.

I have been meditating in a chair since I began my Kriya practice. Before that, I too was in love with the romantic idea that in order to be a real yogi I had to sit cross-legged on the floor. I learned, in time, that it was better for my knees, my back and my meditation practice if I simply sat in a chair.

Also, do not lie down to meditate unless you have a serious medical condition that prevents you from sitting upright. If your back hurts after sitting for extended durations, and it is not due to a serious medical condition, that only indicates you need to exercise to strengthen your core muscles and your back. This too is part of Kriya Yoga practice.

When I first began practicing meditation, I could only sit for 30-45 minutes before my back and shoulders began to ache. I then began to practice Hatha Yoga and strength training. This corrected my posture and strengthened my body so I could sit upright for longer.

If you do have a serious medical condition that requires you to lie down to meditate, then that is what you have to do. Your task will be slightly harder. You will be more inclined to fall asleep and daydream on your back while trying to meditate. It can be done. It just usually takes more effort.

In fact, learning to stay superconscious during sleep is a very important yogic practice. However, it's best advised that one learn to be superconscious in an upright meditation posture before attempting it lying down. More will be said on this in the chapter on yogic sleep.

The Necessity of Detachment

Spiritual teachers and scriptures emphasize the necessity of detachment. Many spiritual seekers misunderstand detachment and think that if they were to actually practice detachment, they would become boring, aloof and withdrawn. This is not so. The purpose of detachment is to give the proper spaciousness and clarity to see one's Self and the nature of the world without conditioning or limitation.

In fact, it is necessary to experience transcendent states. Consider this simple example. Imagine you want to visit California. In order to do this, you have to let go of your attachment to your home in Arkansas. You have to physically detach yourself from your home, property, family, friends, etc. Otherwise, you will never make it to California. The same is true for spiritual realization. You are currently having a human experience, because that is what you are focused on and used to. In order to have a cosmic or "spiritual" experience, you have to let go of attachment to your home, personality, body, friends, history and thoughts, so that you can direct your attention to transcendent realities.

Most people say they want to experience spiritual freedom or cosmic consciousness, but only if they can bring their personality and other life situations with them. It does not work that way. In order to experience spiritual freedom and cosmic consciousness, you have to be able to let go of your limited attachment to the human reality. Detachment and meditation cultivate this potential.

When we meditate, if we are still thinking about the problems in our life, wondering if we got an anticipated correspondence, stopping to check our email, remembering the enjoyable experiences we had yesterday or anything else that may distract us, we will not meditate well, if at all. The purpose of meditation, to know God or your Self, requires that you put down all distractions and focus with intention and devotion on your chosen form of contemplation. If you cannot do this, or will not do this, you might as well take a nap and dream pleasant dreams rather than meditate.

If you cannot do this, that is fine. You can learn to do it. Practicing detachment is not a skill that any of us are born with unless we have already developed it in past lifetimes. Even the best yogis, at some point in their cycle of incarnation, had to learn to do it. It is easy to make excuses and say I cannot meditate. Remember, none of us could do anything until we learned how and then honed the appropriate skill.

If you will not do it, then the practice of Kriya Yoga is not for you. You may still derive stress relief benefits by practicing the techniques and sitting silently for 20 to 30 minutes a day, but if you are not actively honing your capacity to focus and practice detachment, it will not be an enlightening path.

To practice detachment will take a consistent act of your will. It is like developing a muscle or fine motor skill. At first, your muscle may be weak or your nervous system clumsy. But in time, with repetition, the muscle will grow stronger and the nervous system more refined. How do we develop detachment through will power? Here are a few methods I have used with success.

Sitting, Breathing, Watching Procedure

When you first sit to meditate, take some time to observe your internal and external environment. Start with the external environment.

Look around you. What do you see in your environment? Breathe deep. What do you smell? Listen. What sounds do you hear?

Acknowledge the sounds, not to label and judge them as potential distractions, but to simply admit they are there. If you hear a dog barking or a child yelling, simply acknowledge that is your current environment and it may be there with you during meditation.

How does your body feel? Do you feel good or bad? Do you feel tense or relaxed? Where do you feel tension? How do you feel sitting in your meditation seat? The point is to fully acknowledge your external environment, just to admit what is there.

Now that you have taken stock of your external consciousness, look within. What thoughts are your mind consistently thinking? How does your breath feel? What is your current mood? Again, you are doing this, not to judge, just to take stock of your internal consciousness.

Watch your breath. Don't try to deepen it or extend it. Just breathe and watch. Observe the tenacity or intensity of your thoughts. Notice how pressing and serious some thoughts seem. Notice how they keep repeating the same patterns. Just watch.

In time, if you can simply maintain this witnessing presence, not judging, not trying to change anything, just watching the current state of your internal and external consciousness, the distractions will eventually lose their momentum. So long as you can remain alert and attentive, you will find you naturally flow into thought free, superconscious state.

This does take practice, and most people fall asleep as the distractions lose their hold. That is what we have been trained to do. Consciousness clears and relaxes, usually only before we fall asleep. We are training ourselves to remain alert and watchful, while the consciousness relaxes. Then we will experience the tranquility and bliss of the Self as the conditioning thins.

Once you have achieved a relatively quiet and detached state through this practice, you can then engage your meditation techniques and routines with greater success and depth. Meditation techniques themselves can help us experience this state, but I have found that sometimes people practice their techniques while simultaneously caught up in all the distractions around and within them. This is not optimal.

Giving Everything Up to God

Sitting, breathing and watching is a passive approach to achieving detachment. It can be very powerful and effective, but sometimes we need to take a more active approach to achieving detachment without being overly willful or internally violent. The best way to do that is to give up all of your distractions to your concept of the divine.

Remember from the commentary on the Yoga Sutras in *Kriya Yoga: Continuing the Lineage of Enlightenment* that one of the prime practices of Kriya Yoga is surrendering to your concept of the divine. If you cannot do this, you can learn. In fact, it is necessary. If you are living a life without trust, faith or the ability to surrender to the greater mystery of life, you will not be able to derive the full spiritual maturing benefits of Kriya Yoga. How do we apply this to our practice of detachment?

Once again, first sit to meditate. Go through the process of sitting, breathing and watching first. Then acknowledge your concept of the divine. If you could feel it within and around you, what would it feel like? Imagine and acknowledge that presence.

Now, consciously and with active will, affirm that you are giving up all your distractions to the divine. Go through each distraction specifically. Name the distraction and then affirm, "I give this up to the divine, my higher Self." Actually, imagine and visualize what it would feel like if you were releasing that attachment to the divine. Do this for each distraction. Name it. Affirm you are letting it go, and actively imagine and feel that you are doing so.

This may take practice and consistency. At first you may feel foolish and like it is not working. Keep doing it. In time, as the days and months go by, you will see it actually does work. You may also need to be repetitious in a single sitting. For example, you may have a constant concern about a work situation. Each time it comes into your mind, you name the distraction, affirm you are letting it go to the divine, and actively imagine and feel you are doing so. Eventually it will stop bothering you and you will meditate freely.

This will strengthen your consciousness in the same way that maintaining firm boundaries in your daily life will do so. Imagine a troublesome person keeps bothering you. If you consistently affirm your boundaries and disregard that person, eventually they go away. It might take persistence, but it will work. The same applies to your inner troubles. The stronger you are to affirm your boundaries and that your attention is directed to the divine, and not your mundane problems during meditation, in time, no mundane problem will be able to shake your inner tranquility.

Once you have given up all your distractions to the divine, sit in the silence generated, practice your meditation techniques and go deep into your practice. This can be related to any undertaking. When you are trying to learn or accomplish something, you will do a much better job if you can focus your attention on the task at hand rather than trying to fend off distractions. Do what ever you have to, that you may successfully detach your attention from externals and focus on your spiritual work.

Detachment and Integrating Kriya Techniques

You can also utilize your Kriya techniques to improve your capacity for detachment. While you are practicing Kriya Pranayama or Sushumna Breathing, you can visualize each distraction that arises being burned up, disintegrated or dissolved with each repetition.

Imagine you are meditating and practicing Kriya Pranayama, yet your mind is still thinking and thinking. Now, to help calm the mind and facilitate detachment, inhale and imagine that your thoughts are being dissolved and released while that cool soothing electrical current ascends up through the spine. Each repetition will then draw you further internally, and the power of the karmic impressions the thoughts are an expression of will be exhausted.

Tamasic, Rajasic and Sattvic Spiritual Practice

It is important to consider the influences of the Gunas in our meditation practice. Theoretically, the Gunas are three cosmic forces of nature that make our life experience possible. The drama of life ceases when they are in perfect balance. When one Guna predominates over the others, the feeling of incarnation into a separate identity becomes possible.

Traditionally, the Gunas are described thus. Tamas is an energy of darkness, inertia, stability, form, delusion, lack of consideration, dullness, chaos, destruction, apathy and ignorance. Rajas is an energetic quality of activity, transformation, passion, egoism, drive, dissatisfaction, seeking approval and desire for something more. Sattva's quality is peaceful, content, inspired, unified, whole, pure, truth revealing, without craving and tranquil. Any activity or experience you have can be described by a combination of one or more of these energetic threads. All life experiences are woven by the fabric of the Gunas.

In the past, the trouble with Guna theory is the proclivity towards judgmental thinking that it may engender. A ratio of the Gunas makes everything possible. You cannot have a life experience without some combination of these qualities. Even a perceived high spiritual state occurs due to the inspiration of Sattva and the stabilizing quality of Tamas. The dynamic and desirous nature of Rajas is required to motivate one to take up the spiritual path in the first place. Without the destructive nature of Tamas and the drive of Rajas, new advances in understanding would not be possible, as we would ever remain fixed on outdated personal realizations. I say this, only to encourage you to consider that all of the qualities as indicated by the Gunas are necessary, even though we may find some of them less attractive than others.

However, it is the practice of yoga to move our awareness to a primarily Sattvic state. As indicated in the Yoga Sutras of Patanjali, once our life is established in a Sattvic nature and we are able to discern the relationship of the Gunas to Self, then we are on the razor-sharp edge between partial and full Self-realization. It is not the Sattvic nature that causes Self-realization, but the subtle capacity to understand the relationship of the Gunas to the Self. A Sattvic nature makes it easier to perceive this subtle relationship. This is one of the reasons why Kriya Yoga practices paired with Self-inquiry are essential. It is the Kriya Practices that develop our Sattvic state. Then the Self-inquiry provides us the discernment to know what we are in relationship to the Gunas.

When one explores or practices yogic meditation to escape from mental/emotional pain or for healing of any kind, this practice is tamasic. Any time our motivation to act arises from a desire to escape pain or end suffering, it has a tamasic quality to it. There is no judgment in this, and it is perfectly normal. Many people come to spirituality, religion or any self-improvement practice because they are in pain and want to be out of pain.

If one desires to practice meditation to improve a situation or make one's Self better in anyway, this is rajasic. Rajas is the energy of transformation and change. When Rajas dominates, one is often inspired to keep seeking new experiences. You can find Rajas dominating in highly functional, determined meditators, who may say they are seeking to realize the Self or God, but are really only trying to validate an incessant need to be better or prove themselves. This is common in individuals who focus on doing more meditation or spiritual practice, versus spending time focusing on improving the quality of practice.

In Rajas, it can be hard to settle into a simple yet effective practice of meditation, because one always thinks there must be a better technique out there to give one a better experience. Many people, who focus primarily on technique, are caught up in Rajas. Technique has its place, but is not the key to final realization. It is a part of the whole process. In a Rajasic state, the focus is on having experiences and making ourselves better.

Sattva, being the energy of peace, contentment and tranquility, inspires one to meditate, not because one is in pain or feels the need to be better or have better experiences, but out of pure and simple inspiration to sit still and quiet in what is. Sattva predominates when you can sit quietly, ask the question, "God would you please reveal your self to me?" and then you can sit and realize, with great joy, that God is the chair in which you are sitting. God is the bird song outside. God is the light through the room. God is your breath, your thoughts, your body, and the space in which all these perceived things occur. And that is enough and even more than enough. This is in comparison to a Rajasic meditation where one expects God to show up, as has been explained in fantastic stories of sages and saints in popular culture. So you see, our ideal is not to reach or immerse our Self in God, but to learn to see the actual reality of that which we call God!

We know our *motivations* are sattvic when our reason for taking action arises out of inspiration and joy. We do the thing, only because it is natural to us. There is no need for reward, recognition or validation. We do it because we want to and enjoy it. Consider an activity you engage in regularly, that you do because you love it, not because you want someone to see you doing it or because you will be rewarded in any way for doing it. This is an example of a Sattvic activity and *any* activity can be Sattvic. Some people take up meditation for this reason. They can't help it. It's joyful. They do not do it because a perceived authority figure said it will burn away sins, or allow one to be a good and spiritual person. They do it only because it is natural.

The more we engage our spiritual practice, being ever vigilant about our motivations, we can move into Sattvic meditation. You know when your inner work is Sattvic when you do it because you truly love it and cannot help but do it. You no longer sit to meditate because someone told you it's good for you or will get you into heavenly states. When you miss a practice session, you don't feel guilty because you have failed to be a good yogi, you feel sad, because you missed out on something you really enjoy and love. There is a major difference in these approaches.

Please remember, that if you or any person is in an inert, dull, ignorant or painful state and seeks to escape that state through meditation or spiritual practice, this is perfectly fine and natural. The reasons why we begin our journey to realization does not matter, so long as we engage it from where we are. Also, it is perfectly fine to practice with Rajasic intentions. If you practice because you feel you will be a better person for practicing, at least you are practicing. That is what is most important. This will help to improve our practices and make us more skillful. The problem with Rajas is when we focus more on the doing itself and doing more to be better. We need the will and drive of Rajas to motivate us to stay alert and awake while we meditate and learn to settle into an inspired, tranquil Sattvic state. With time and attention, we can establish ourself in a Sattvic meditative state with less and less motivation to escape pain (Tamas), and less personal effort (Rajas). Although, in the beginning, painful motivation and personal effort are perfectly necessary.

Meditation and what most people consider spiritual practice is actually very easy and simple. In fact, it is so simple and easy, we can't believe it. Therefore, we get caught up in Rajas. If we are to trust those who have made the way before us, we can realize that our doing is helpful, yet after we do, we learn to settle into Sattva, surrender and be at peace with what is. The more comfortable this becomes, the more inspired our life and meditations will be.

Then any activity can be Sattvic, which is particularly important to remember. Why? Because Sattva is often interpreted to mean that a person will do everything perfectly and act holy and pious at all times. Many people act perfect, holy and pious out of Rajas motivations. It is much better to be yourself, because it is natural and enjoyable. To force yourself into a perceived Sattvic role or image, because a culture or authority has made you believe it will make you a better person, is a certain way to pain and ignorance.

To paraphrase, your ultimate goal is to learn to stay alert and attentive, yet relaxed and content throughout your life and meditation practice. Take action as you are called to, and surrender to the rest of it.

Why Do I Share the Kriya Techniques Freely?

If you have wondered why I am sharing these techniques so freely, this is a good question to ask. It is one I am happy to answer. Do be aware I have alluded to my reasons previously in the chapter on GURU AND INITIATION. However, I will repeat myself, in a different manner, so that it is very clear. Clarity is important and so is repetition.

For many centuries, Kriya procedures have been guarded and reserved only for those who participate in Kriya Initiations or dedicate their life to a guru lineage and Kriya tradition. This was an important way to preserve the tradition and teachings as we came out of the Kali Yuga (the Dark Ages, roughly 400 A.D. to 1600 A.D.).

Over the last two centuries, we have seen Kriya teachings evolve from being taught secretly, during quiet personal initiations, to large group teachings and initiations. According to our known history of Kriya, students were taught directly by Mahavatar Babaji to his disciples, who had renounced the world to travel and be with him.

Then Lahiri Mahasaya was encouraged to practice Kriya as a householder, who would raise a family, work in the world while simultaneously meditating and teaching at night to other householders, as well as yogis. Lahiri Mahasaya had many disciples and a few students who were qualified to teach. They continued the lineage and tradition. (Remember, there are numerous branches of Kriya Yoga, and one is not better than another. You simply find the one best suited to your temperament.)

One of Lahiri Mahasaya's students, Swami Sri Yukteswar, took on the task of preparing Paramahansa Yogananda, who would take Kriya Yoga teachings to the Western world. At this time, he is perhaps the most well known teacher to have introduced Kriya Yoga to America. Yogananda was well trained and told by Swami Sri Yukteswar to teach Kriya Yoga with an emphasis on the *Yoga Sutras of Patanjali*.

Paramahansa Yogananda would continue the tradition of teaching householders how to practice Kriya and experience Self and God-realization. He also started an organization (Self-Realization Fellowship) to support monastics in their dharma of renunciation.

Paramahansa also gave large-scale initiations, which was in contrast to the one-on-one initiations of his predecessors. Yogananda, in turn, had a few well known and some unknown disciples who he would instruct and empower to continue the tradition and initiate others into Kriya. The three most well-known of Yogananda's students, who would continue the tradition outside of the Self-Realization Fellowship confines, were Donald Walters (Swami Kriyananda), Oliver Black and Roy Eugene Davis. All three began their own organizations to continue sharing the authentic Kriya practices of their particular lineage through time.

Mr. Davis met Yogananda and was initiated when he was in his late teens. A few years later Mr. Davis would be empowered and instructed to teach Kriya by Yogananda. Mr. Davis did just that. His organization, Center for Spiritual Awareness, has been steadily continuing Yogananda's work since the 1970s.

I met Mr. Davis in late summer of 2000, when I was initiated by him. I was later ordained as a minister of his organization, empowered and authorized to teach in the Summer of 2005. (Please see the book *Kriya Yoga: Continuing the Lineage of Enlightenment* for more details.) From 2000 onward, as I practiced Kriya privately every day, attended retreats two to three times a year, met with Mr. Davis often and worked with individuals and groups teaching Kriya Yoga, I began to have a few important realizations.

My first realization began to develop around the winter of 2007. I had increased my time spent in meditation that fall and had begun studying and contemplating the *Talks of Ramana Maharshi* and the book *Vasistha's Yoga*. Through this intensification of my practice, I began to have the sense that the guru was not a person, but the very nature of pure consciousness itself.

I began to lose my desire to attune to any particular person or lineage, but to acknowledge the divine presence, infinite pure consciousness, whatever you want to call it, as the very foundation for all time and space, objectivity and subjectivity. It felt as though my core, my very being, from my petty personality clear through to my highest Self, was actually an expression of a seamless timeless whole. I also began to have the sense that everyone, every experience, every book, every lecture and every moment in quiet contemplation was an expression of the divine infinite and the guru. This did not make me feel special or important. In fact, it had the opposite effect. Everything appeared to be a manifestation of a seemingly diversified wholeness. Nothing was special, yet everything was beautiful and full of awe.

This was a strange sensation for someone who was very devoted (some might say fanatical) and dedicated to his tradition and teacher. I had felt that *my* Kriya tradition was the correct one. I had felt that *my* Kriya teacher was the best one. And now, at home meditating, instead of attuning to the guru lineage of Mahavatar Babaji, Lahiri Mahasaya, Sri Yukteswar, Paramahansa Yogananda and Roy Eugene Davis, I would simply acknowledge that divine light that was within me as my very Self and that divine light that was within all beings, as the guru.

Since I was a teacher for a particular organization, I continued in the way I had been taught. When I initiated others, I would do so as a vessel for the Kriya lineage of which I was a part. When I would begin a meditation, I would encourage others to attune to that particular lineage. It seemed fine to me. It was easier than trying to explain how I felt the guru as everyone and everything I encountered, including the people looking to learn Kriya from me. This continued for a few years.

The next realization also came upon me slowly. I began to observe all of the people who would attend the Kriya retreats I attended. I went to many, so I had a chance to observe many different populations of people who were being initiated into and practicing Kriya. There were many people older than myself and a few younger. Some had been practicing for many decades, some only a few months. Some were new age, some were professional, successful, well-groomed and wealthy, some were poor, some were intelligent, and some were just looking for the next spiritual fad to try. I also began to meet people from other lineages, and I would pay attention to them. The diversity of spiritual seekers was vast. I took special notice of those who would attend my own classes and whom I would initiate. I was curious to see how the process was working for each of them, and what those who had the best results might be doing.

I should also add, that about this time we moved to Asheville, N.C., which is full of every kind of spirituality, meditation group and spiritual teacher you can imagine. Because of this, I took my survey beyond Kriya practitioners. I began to observe other spiritual teachers and their way. I observed their adherents. I began to observe the spiritual depth of those who practiced other kinds of meditation. I was curious. Who was making the most progress? Who could talk about spirituality, but had no realization. Who actually embodied and radiated the peace of the Self without words? Who was winning the spiritual game to reach Self-realization first!? This continued for three years.

During those three years, I made nine important observations.

1. The teacher a spiritual seeker was devoted to had little noticeable effect on the seeker's spiritual progress or state of consciousness. I observed, had conversations with and was "talked at" by many.

2. The particular method of meditation, be it Kriya, Zen, Transcendental Meditation, Christian Contemplation, etc., did not have any special influence in regards to the seeker's spiritual progress or state of consciousness.

3. People initiated into Kriya (from any Kriya organization), and those who were not, were equally likely to be a confused mess of spiritual jargon, as they were to be serene and Self-realized.

4. Those who understood the mechanics, purpose and value of meditation and healthy living, and practiced

superconscious contemplation daily, were more likely to be at peace inside and aware of their connection to the wholeness of life. This was true of those who were initiated into Kriya, as well as those who were not. It was equally true for those who practiced other styles of meditation or spiritual growth, too.

5. Those who practiced their meditation and spirituality, not to escape from problems (tamasic reasons) or to make themselves better (rajasic reasons), but to understand what they are at the core of their being and their relationship to the wholeness of life, were more likely to be content and show signs of Self-realization. This was true no matter what style of meditation they practiced, who initiated them, or if they were initiated into a spiritual path at all.

6. Those who were not seeking a group to belong to, or a teacher to fill a pseudo parent role, but were looking for the tools and methods to help them grow to full maturity usually showed the signs of peace and Self-realization more readily.

7. Those who were seeking the quick-fix-rocket-ship-path-to-enlightenment by learning Kriya Pranayama rarely stayed the course long enough to derive any benefit. If they did stay the course, they were usually distracted by fanatically trying to tell people how good their path was, rather than actually practicing it.

8. Those who saw the Kriya methods and philosophy as an intelligently designed process, that if applied consistently and with patience over the course of their

life, were more likely to demonstrate signs of Self-realization and peace. This was true for those who had been initiated, as well as those who had simply read about the practices and began applying them on their own. This was also true for those who treated other paths with the same understanding and respect.

9. There was a large population of people who were interested in practicing Kriya and meditation but were completely turned off by organizations requiring pledges of unfailing loyalty, outrageous fees to learn a simple mantra practice and subsequently, teachers who would only teach if the person swore allegiance to them as their only source of spiritual information.

When all of these observations came together in my mind, something strong began to grow inside. When I led meditation at the center where I was Senior Minister, I had a hard time continuing to ask participants to only attune to a specific guru lineage. (It was about this time that I parted from the organization, with Mr. Davis' encouragement, to be an independent teacher and to follow my inner guidance.) I had difficulty professing that this Kriya path was the only and best way. Instead, at the beginning of meditations, I began to encourage participants to honor those teachers who they learned from. After all, if it wasn't for their teacher's own life's work and practice, we would not have had all the information we do about spiritual practices today. I also encouraged them to honor and acknowledge that divine light within themselves, which is the same light in every spiritual personage. I made it a point that honoring that light, within each and everyone one of us, was more important than devotion to one particular person we deem as spiritual. If everything is

God, which it is, then how can something or someone be more God than something or someone else? It may be someone acts more like we think a spiritual person should, but again, if everything and everyone is God, than that's it. Period.

Now, I must admit here that I do see the value in having such devotion for another person (be it a guru, spouse, friend, etc.), or even a strong sense of devotion to one's imagined image of a God or Goddess. It is valuable because it allows us, or gives us an excuse, as I like to say, to feel a sense of awe and love because of devotion to some *thing*. This is good. And not everyone is psychologically, mentally or emotionally ready to admit responsibility for their own capacity to feel and be awe and love, the primary indications of Self-realization. That is fine, too. We are all on the spectrum. However, if you are reading this, then time, space and circumstance are showing you the truth of the matter.

If we can start to feel that awe, respect and honor for a person we see as spiritual, or a concept of the divine, it means we can eventually begin to feel it for no reason. This is ideal. If we can feel it for no reason, then no reason can take it away. So to be fair, devotion to a guru or image of the divine is a stepping stone on the Self-realization path and very helpful. The problem arises when we don't recognize it as a stepping stone and get hung up on only being able to feel that sense of awe, joy and fulfillment when we are in the presence of our guru, or on retreat, or praying to our imagined concept of the divine. It's always there, whether you allow yourself to admit it or not.

Always remember, you can only feel, experience or realize something if it is already within you! My goal is not to encourage you to give up your enjoyable devotion to a person, path or thing. You can continue to enjoy it. My goal is to help you see it for what it is, not a source for your peace and Self-realization, but an excuse to experience it while you play your role in the world. When you feel more comfortable, or your spiritual practice has ripened you enough, you will then happily acknowledge that your Self-realization, peace and contentment was your very Self all along. Then you will not need to be with anyone, go anywhere, or believe in anything to experience it. Enjoy the process, but don't get stuck at the stage of devotion to an object. And yes, people are objects. Unless, of course, you admit they are not objects, which would make them simply another facet of your very Self after all.

To return to my original point, it was the combinations of the above-mentioned realizations and observations that inspired me to teach as I now do, and to share Kriya in this manner, freely and openly. As with all things, Kriya has evolved from being practiced by a secret cult of practitioners in the Himalayas, to being shared quietly with householders in the late 19th century, to being taught through large organizations throughout the 20th century, to now being available to those individuals with the capacity to understand the philosophy and practice the techniques intelligently on their own.

Even though I have realized that the Kriya path is not special, nor is any person more divine than anyone else, I appreciate the simplicity, practicality and effectiveness of the process. To be very clear, the Kriya Yoga process works very well. Because of this, I am even more devoted to the techniques and philosophy.

It is my goal to inspire others who are similarly interested to take up the task of working out their own Self-realization. It is my goal to encourage them to explore and apply the process with a clear head, free of fantasy, and with a realistic understanding of what is required to actually experience Self-realization. It is my goal to encourage Kriya practitioners to honor the men and women who have served as a torchbearer for this work, to seek out their counsel, writings or lectures when necessary, but not to be dependent on them. The Self in all spiritual personages is the same Self that is within you, all time, space and beyond. It is my goal to give you an excuse to realize this, until you no longer need an excuse and it becomes as natural as breathing.

Chapter Six

KRIYA MEDITATION ROUTINES

Your time in meditation is sacred. It is during your chosen meditation time that you are able to consciously withdraw from the world of form and redirect the attention of your soul back to the eternal, timeless nature of your pure being. It is this pure being that is the support and foundation for every experience you have ever had. It is the support for the physical reality you experience now and at any and every moment in the past. It is the support for your mental realities, your thoughts, ideas, opinions and preferences. It is the support for every dream or nightmare. It is the screen on which every emotion shines, be it love, sadness, despair, joy, anxiety, fear, apathy, disgust, compassion, awe, gratitude, lust, rapture, hatred, contentment, confidence, etc. Pure being is the source, support and innate substance of every experience. Our spiritual practice removes the obstacles that allow us to realize this fact.

It is for this reason that we spoke of detachment as a necessary skill for any devoted Kriya Yogi. Through the practice and mastery of detachment, we can make our meditation times as sacred as possible. By practicing detachment — consciously releasing our awareness of the incessant thoughts in our mind, disregarding the replay of all our old useless memories, ignoring the worry about all the feelings and circumstances we cannot control — we are able to truly worship and commune with pure being. We choose to put our full attention on the infinite timeless consciousness that people often refer to as divine. As long as we give attention to our endless capacity for distractions, we cannot rest our attention in the divine presence.

Notice that I did not say detachment requires that you stop thinking, or stop having memories, or stop feeling. I said you release or disregard these things. The mind cannot be stopped any more than the world of form can be annihilated. The mind and creation are an eternal aspect of the manifested aspect of consciousness. There is no end to it, just as there is no beginning. However, we can redirect our attention to subtler realms or experientially attenuated aspects of consciousness.

Imagine you are at home focused on an important project for work. Now imagine your cat keeps jumping on your lap, your friends keep calling, your spouse is cooking a dinner that requires she use a very loud blender. However, you need to focus on your work. Through the practice of detachment, you can withdraw your senses to focus only on the task at hand. Then you become unaware of all these distractions and you are fully absorbed in your work. The world of form continues doing what it does, but you train yourself to focus your awareness on what is important.

Meditation works the same way. Your mind may continue thinking, but you don't have to listen. You can listen to it later when it is appropriate to think. You may still have your underlying emotional state that is specific to you as a personality, yet you can train yourself to forget about it for a while, until it is appropriate to play that role again. This takes practice and it is usually not easy. Due to the amount of time it takes, most people quit and say they can't meditate. This is mainly due to the fact that most meditation schools, who try to tout their approach as the best, claim that you should be able to stop your thoughts and internalize your attention to experience peace by using their method after only a short time. Now, if you already have the capacity to direct your attention to peace and clarity, this will probably be true for you. However, most of us need to practice this.

As with all skills, as the months and years go by, you refine your capacity to meditate. What was once difficult or strenuous now becomes easy and fluid. I like to say that you know you are skillful in meditation when you look forward to it, and the silence that is revealed, as you would look forward to a hot, relaxing bath on cold, bitter winter's day. A solid meditation routine, which you can count on, provides the proper foundation for this to occur.

Creating a Sacred Space

All time and space is sacred, but before most people can fully realize that, it helps to consciously declare a certain time or space sacred. By choosing to meditate at the same time every day, and in the same place every day, you start to create a sacred space. It helps if you consciously declare this certain time and space as something sacred.

Think of a time when you had a meeting with a person you deeply loved or respected. Or remember a time when you entered a sacred site. Before you met this person or entered that site, your mind and emotions probably generated a sense reverence, awe and specialness. I doubt you were thinking about your bills, how you were abused as a child, or the problems you have at work. You were fully absorbed in the anticipation of connecting to the energy of that person or site. You can remember that feeling and actively draw forth that same sense when you think about or enter the sacred time and space of your meditation.

The combination of consciously drawing forth the feeling of sacredness and the very act of meditation itself will enliven the environment and that specific time period you have chosen. This makes it easier to meditate there and then. The mind is more easily ignored because your consciousness knows that when you sit down in that location and at that time, your attention is meant to flow into superconscious awareness.

Some people need props to invoke the sense of awe and sacredness. When I was younger, I loved getting up early, going into a dark room, lighting my favorite incense, and lighting a candle in my favorite lotus candleholder. I loved wrapping myself in a wool blanket and taking five to ten minutes to simply gaze at the photos before me of the people I considered enlightened. I loved the feeling of the rudraksha mala in my hands. All this gave me a sense of sacredness. When I meditated with all of these props, I was in another time and space where all my normal life distractions did not matter.

As time passed, this became less and less necessary. I still enjoy and love to create a space like that, particularly when I am meditating with others. I also enjoy visiting a meditation center or someone else's home to meditate, and I appreciate any rituals or props they may have to set the tone. However, now on my own, I sit in my plain chair with no special props or ritual, close my eyes and off it goes. It doesn't matter to me if I can hear kids playing outside, or the full sun is shining through the windows. Light or dark, noisy or otherwise, it really doesn't matter. It was not always this way, and practicing with the necessary props for as long as I needed them was essential. So you see, we also evolve over time in our own needs for a sacred meditation space.

For those who are just beginning this path, I would say do everything you can to meditate at the same time every day. Do everything you can or need to that will make you feel a sense of the sacred. By doing this, you will increase the likelihood that you will continue your practice over the years.

Commit to the time you choose. Make it important for meditation. Don't say, I'll meditate at this time and then give contingencies. Make your meditation practice a high priority over most other things. If you are scheduled to meditate at 4 a.m. or 6 a.m. in the morning, that is your sacred time. Remember this when your friends ask you out for a late evening. It may be that you decline the evening date. What is more important to you? Your meditation and spiritual exploration, or your late nights out? It may be that your social life is more important, and that is fine. Let's just be clear about that. But if Self-realization is your highest priority, then discipline and sacrifice will be necessary.

When I first began this process, I even stopped sleeping in the same bed with my wife for nearly a year. Why did I do this? Because I set my time for meditation during early morning hours. I noticed that when I slept in the same bed with her, I had a very hard time getting up and going to meditate. The bed was warm and comfortable and dreaming was sweet. However, it was most important for me to meditate, so I told her I will be sleeping in the other room so I can get up early. After some misunderstood and hurt feelings, she consented. For the next year, I was able to get up easily and get right to meditation. It was not that I loved her any less, but it was that my spiritual practice had higher priority. In time, I trained myself to get up and meditate whether I was sleeping alone or with my wife. Thankfully, as the years passed, I was forgiven, as she later clearly understood my reasons.

Creating a sacred time and space for meditation sets the stage for an effective meditation routine.

The Basic Pattern of Meditation

Over the years, as my capacity to meditate deepened and lengthened, I have followed one basic pattern. I have not deviated from this pattern since I began practicing meditation. I have taken note of this pattern and shared it repeatedly, because I have noticed that one of the major obstacles most meditators seem to have is the inability to structure an effective meditation session based on their current skill level. Let's start with the basic pattern and then we will develop it for beginner, intermediate and advanced Kriya practitioners.

Step 1: Before entering my sacred space, I decide which meditation techniques I will be utilizing today. This way, I won't have to wonder about it. I know the process I intend to do before I begin.

Step 2: I enter the sacred space and sit comfortably and upright. I take a moment to become aware of my surroundings. I pay attention to all the input coming into my senses. I pay attention to how I feel in my body and mind. I just observe and acknowledge.

Step 3: If I have a ritual, such as lighting incense or a candle or gazing at images of people or divinities I consider enlightened, I do so.

Step 4: I take an easy, deep breath. Exhale and relax. I close my eyes and turn my attention within.

Step 5: I acknowledge the innate divinity within and around me. I acknowledge the innate divine nature of all people, places and things. (If you are attached to a guru, it can be a good time to acknowledge that person's positive connection in your life.) I feel as though I am not a limited personality, but feel that I am infinite consciousness and that every breath, moment, thought, feeling and experience is an expression of the wholeness of life.

Step 6: I begin my chosen meditation technique, typically alternate nostril breathing or mantra. I will continue this technique either until I have completed the set number of repetitions or until I feel my consciousness serene and internalized.

Step 7: I will sit quietly with my attention in the higher brain centers for as long as the internalized serenity lasts. I simply sit, watch and observe.

Step 8: I repeat Steps 6 and 7 two or three more times. This depends on how many techniques I have decided to practice.

Step 9: I once again imagine all of consciousness as an expression of one whole infinite seamless being. I imagine and see all the people, places, things and situations in my life imbued with the sense of serenity, peace and Self-knowledge. I then expand awareness to include all beings in all times in every realm. I see them as an expression of my very Self. I see them imbued with that same sense of love, fulfillment and Self-knowledge.

Step 10: When I feel ready (or my timer goes off), I open my eyes and go about my day.

BEGINNER MEDITATION ROUTINES

New Kriya Yoga practitioners will aim for a 30-minute meditation session once or twice a day.

Beginning Meditation Routine

Step 1: Assume your chosen meditation posture. Practice the *Sitting, Breathing, Watching Procedure* mentioned previously.

Step 2: Honor and acknowledge the innate divine presence within and around you. Feel yourself one with the wholeness of life. Feel, acknowledge and imagine the same capacity for Self-realization that you see in people you consider enlightened as a light within your heart, shining as your very Self. Imagine that in whatever way you can.

Step 3: Practice a simple mantra technique for five to ten minutes.

Step 4: After the mantra practice, sit quietly with your attention at the spiritual eye center or crown. Rest in whatever tranquility or peace has been revealed. Keep in mind, if you are a new practitioner, you may still be having thoughts, and distractions arise. However, notice that you are less engaged in them. Even after only five to ten minutes of practice, your mind will be a little calmer and your consciousness a little clearer. Rest in that.

Step 5: Practice the *Kriya Life Force Arousal Technique*.

Step 6: Practice *Kriya Pranayama* technique.

Step 7: Endeavor to hold your attention at the spiritual eye or crown center, sitting in the stillness, for five to ten minutes. Most people find this very easy to do after practicing Kriya Pranayama. You may even find you can sit in the stillness for longer than 10 minutes. As long as you are awake (not being passive and daydreaming), relaxed yet watchful, you can remain in this state for as long as you like.

Step 8: Practice *Jyoti Mudra*.

Step 9: After sitting in the silence revealed through Jyoti Mudra, take some time for quiet prayer. By prayer, I don't mean asking God or the Universe to fulfill your personal desires. I mean to acknowledge and invite a deeper communion with your Self, pure infinite consciousness. Also, take some time to consider all the blessings in your life. See all people, places and things in your life filled with this same sense of gratitude and wonder.

Step 10: Open your eyes and go about your day.

This basic meditation routine can be extended by including periods of reflection on spiritual literature. For example, after practicing Kriya Pranayama and sitting in the stillness, instead of going directly to Jyoti Mudra, you can read a few paragraphs or pages of an inspiring spiritual book. Then before concluding with quiet prayer, you can repeat the process. Reflect on the meaning of the verses you have read. Sit quietly a few more minutes and then practice Step 9 and 10.

Extending your meditation in this way once or twice a week is ideal. Remember though, the main focus of meditation is to learn to internalize your attention and to exist in pure consciousness. The addition of reading spiritual literature is only to help you, as a beginner, to sit longer and stay focused on your contemplative time. Only do this when you have time and are happy to sit longer, engaging your spiritual practice.

KRIYA YOGA VICHARA

INTERMEDIATE MEDITATION ROUTINES

Intermediate Kriya Practitioners can now engage the process for 45 to 75 minutes once or twice a day. Aim to begin this process after six months to a year of practicing the beginner routine.

Step 1: Assume your chosen meditation posture. Practice the *Sitting, Breathing, Watching Procedure* mentioned previously, or any of the routines previously described to help with detachment during meditation.

Step 2: Honor and acknowledge the innate divine presence within and around you. Feel yourself one with the wholeness of life. Feel, acknowledge and imagine the same capacity for Self-realization that you see in people you consider enlightened as a light within your heart, shining as your very Self. Imagine that in whatever way you can.

Step 3: Practice Nadi Shodhana (alternate nostril breathing) for 12 to 24 rounds.

Step 4: Rest in the silence for two to three minutes with eyes closed. Hold your awareness on your body and your breath, observing the current state of your consciousness.

Step 5: Practice the *Kriya Life Force Arousal Technique*.

Step 6: Practice *Kriya Pranayama* technique.

Step 7: Endeavor to hold your attention at the spiritual eye or crown center, sitting in the stillness, for 10 to 15 minutes. As long as you are awake (not being passive and daydreaming), relaxed yet watchful, you can remain in this state for as long as you like.

Step 8: Practice *Jyoti Mudra*.

Step 9: After sitting for an extended period of time in the silence generated by Jyoti Mudra, you can practice an additional meditation technique from this book to refresh and deepen your practice. Chanting through the chakras, gentle sushumna breathing, 2nd Tier Kriya Practice or mantra practice are best.

Step 9.5: (Optional) Practice listening to and absorbing yourself into the Om vibration.

Step 10: After sitting in the silence generated by your additional chosen meditation technique, take some time for quiet prayer. Also, take some time to consider all the blessings in your life. See all people, places, and things in your life filled with this same sense of gratitude and wonder.

Step 11: Open your eyes and go about your day.

Intermediate practitioners will also benefit by including periods of contemplation (see later chapter). This can be done after Kriya Pranayama and before Jyoti Mudra. It can be done after Jyoti Mudra and before Step 9. It can be done in between Step 9 and 10. Or if you are feeling exceptionally inspired and spiritually energetic, you can practice it at all three intervals.

Always remember though, the purpose is not to keep your mind and consciousness engaged with techniques or contemplation. The magick of meditation occurs when you are aware of your pure being, your Self. Meditation techniques and contemplation help to keep you focused and intent. If we find we are easily able to experience the silence and totality of our pure infinite consciousness, we disregard contemplation and techniques and rest in that experience. We continue with techniques and contemplation only so long as we need them.

As an intermediate practitioner, aim to sit in meditation for 90 minutes once a week. Do this on a day when you have less mundane responsibilities and can easily schedule the additional meditation time. This will give you a chance to explore deeper aspects of your practice by learning to extend your time sitting in the silence.

ADVANCED MEDITATION ROUTINES

Advanced Kriya meditators can practice meditation for 75 minutes to two hours once or twice a day.

However, it is important to note that as an advanced meditator, you actually don't have to sit for longer. When we reach an advanced stage of meditation we go deeper into the practice quicker, and we can stay there more easily. We also are more likely to remain superconscious throughout our daily interactions. Advanced meditators are probably also practicing superconscious sleep (see chapter on Yogic Sleep). In this way, an advanced meditator does not usually require a forced routine of lengthy meditations.

I say this, so you don't get the idea that the longer you meditate the better. Again, quality is better than quantity. A beginning meditator may spend the entire 30 minutes of his or her practice getting a handle on how to practice technique effectively and only spend five minutes in quiet stillness. An advanced meditator may be able to access that stillness after only a few Kriya Pranayamas, and he or she may spend 30 to 60 minutes absorbed in pure consciousness.

Complexity and length of practice does not equate to an advanced meditation session. In my mind, the more techniques and complexity we need, the less advanced we are in our practice. An advanced meditator is one who can easily turn attention within and exist in pure being.

For the sake of method, the following "advanced" procedures can be utilized as needed. Even advanced meditators need a routine and formalized practice from time to time to keep them engaged.

Step 1: Assume your chosen meditation posture. Practice the *Sitting, Breathing, Watching Procedure* mentioned previously, or any of the routines previously described to help with detachment during meditation.

Step 2: Honor and acknowledge the innate divine presence within and around you. Feel yourself one with the wholeness of life. Feel, acknowledge and imagine the same capacity for Self-realization that you see in people you consider enlightened as a light within your heart, shining as your very Self. Imagine that in whatever way you can.

Step 3: Practice Nadi Shodhana (alternate nostril breathing) for 24 rounds. (This is optional, although I find it very helpful and begin all of my meditations this way. If you like, mantra meditation for 15 minutes can be substituted.)

Step 4: Rest in the silence for 10 minutes with eyes closed. Hold your awareness on your body and your breath, observing the current state of your consciousness.

Step 5: Practice the *Kriya Life Force Arousal Technique*.

Step 6: Practice *Kriya Pranayama* technique.

Step 7: Endeavor to hold your attention at the spiritual eye or crown center, sitting in the stillness, for 15 minutes. As long as you are awake (not being passive and daydreaming), relaxed yet watchful, you can remain in this state for as long as you like.

Step 8: Practice *Jyoti Mudra*.

Step 9: After sitting for an extended period of time in the silence generated by Jyoti Mudra, you can practice the 2nd Tier Kriya Practice.

Step 10: After sitting for an extended period of time in the silence generated by the 2nd Tier Kriya Practice, you can take up the 3rd Tier Kriya Practice. (If you have already been practicing the 3rd Tier Practice for six months to a year, then use the 4th Tier Kriya Practice instead.)

Step 11: Practice contemplation.

Step 11.5: (Optional) Practice listening to and absorbing yourself into the Om vibration.

Step 12: After sitting in the silence, take some time for quiet prayer. Also, take some time to consider all the blessings in your life. See all people, places, and things in your life filled with this same sense of gratitude and wonder.

Step 13: Open your eyes and go about your day.

Time limits can sometimes be constraining to our meditation practice. The suggested times given above are for promoting a methodical approach only. As you become more proficient, the less you have to worry about time.

I have found that on days when I had more free time, if I sat to meditate without any set time restrictions, I often meditate much deeper and for much longer than I usually do with no trouble at all. If I would usually set my timer for one hour of meditation, and instead just meditate without thought for time or duration, I would often find myself sitting for two to two and a half hours easily. The time would fly by and I would still be fully engaged in the process.

Try this once a week. Do not have a set duration for your meditation. Do this on a day when you have nothing else to do, worry about or attend to. Then see how easy it is to sit for longer and to go deeper into the practice when time is not a concern.

Absorption In Om

As you become comfortable existing in the silence of pure being, you may become more and more aware of the Om vibration. This can occur at any time during meditation, although it usually occurs as one becomes more settled into their practice. When this arises, do your best to pay attention to the sound of Om and endeavor to merge your sense of Self within that vibration. The *Inner Light and Sound Technique* is under the section for beginner practices but is actually one of the most advanced and hardest to master. It is also the most rewarding.

This is listed as optional under the intermediate and advanced sections, because it is not something we want to force. It will happen naturally. If you try to force hearing and absorption in Om, it will only generate frustration and make one more likely to stop the process. When it does occur, pay attention.

RYAN KURCZAK

INSIGHTS INTO THE KRIYA PROCESS

The Breathless State

After practicing Kriya Pranayama and Jyoti Mudra, some do not feel the need to breathe as deeply or as often. This is natural. It is not necessarily the "breathless state" that many spiritual seekers long for or glamorize.

When the mind is very calm and we are superconscious, the body may seem to stop breathing or to breathe imperceptibly. This is natural, too. It can be likened to the breathless state. These moments of suspension of breathing may last a few minutes or even longer.

Most yogis do not actually know when they go into a breathless state, because the mind is so calm and consciousness so serene that body awareness is lost in favor of attention on pure being. This state cannot be generated by holding one's breath. It develops over time as one's practice matures. It is not to be sought as a goal. It is to happen naturally when one's consciousness is ready for it.

To help mature one's practice, the following technique can be employed. Again, the goal is not to experience the breathless state, but to internalize the attention so completely and peacefully, that if the breathless state is accessible, it will be experienced. Do the following practice once or twice a week.

After Kriya Pranayama, Jyoti Mudra or the higher tiers of practice, give your attention to your entire body. Feel the extent of the body from the head to the toes, from the spine to the skin. Try to feel it all. Then, using the gentle force of your will, imagine you are pulling in your life force from the extremities, through the nerves into your spine. Create a system for yourself that allows you to visualize this effectively. I like to imagine my spine is generating a vacuum that suctions in the outgoing energies of my senses and the life force in my nerves.

Once you confidently feel or imagine you have withdrawn your life force from your body into the spine, then slowly and gently imagine you are pulling that life force up to the spiritual eye and crown center. Rest with the feeling that all of your senses have been internalized and all of your life force has been withdrawn into the spine and then up into the spiritual eye and crown. Stay in this state for as long as possible.

With practice, you will catch small moments of breathlessness and profound being. This will increase in duration as your practice matures.

Memories, Feelings and Thoughts

Our minds constantly bombard our awareness with thoughts, memories and feelings. What is the source of these sometimes intrusive distractions? They are the result of experiences you have not processed or properly digested. When we rest or take time to meditate, that is a perfect time for these memories, thoughts and feelings to try and find resolution. This is why many people have difficulty falling asleep, because their mind will not stop. This is also why so many people claim they cannot meditate. They say their mind will not shut down.

When we first learn to meditate, our goal is to learn how to sit up, alert and watchful, while simultaneously relaxing our body, mind and consciousness. Most people are trained to go to sleep when the body relaxes. Our first task in meditation is to stay awake and conscious while relaxing. After this is achieved, a person will then be able to stay awake, but now the mind seizes the moment to bring up any undigested memories or experiences in the form of an incessant stream of thoughts. The cure is patience, non-judgment and the capacity to remain as the detached witness of these thoughts for the duration of your practice in which they persist.

This is one of the most important stages of meditation, and the stage where most people give up, saying they cannot meditate. These memories, thoughts and feelings need to be processed. When we practice meditation and a sudden rush of mental distractions arise, that is a good sign. It means your consciousness has shifted into neutral. Your task now is to remain alert, yet relaxed, and watch those thoughts pass from a detached or disinterested perspective. The trouble arises when you engage the thoughts or overthink them, rather than simply watching. Imagine the thoughts are like the clouds passing through the sky. Just watch them pass. Do not worry how long it's going to take. It will take as long as it needs to.

When you do this, you are exhausting the strength of those thoughts. In time, (maybe days, weeks or months depending on how much internal baggage you have), the mind will be clear, relieved of all the unprocessed experiences or memories. Then after you practice a meditation technique, you will experience that alert, relaxed, present moment, which you imagine true meditation to be. Do bear in mind that the stage of learning to let the thoughts pass, while you watch from an alert, relaxed and disinterested vantage point, is a key step in experiencing thought-free meditation. It is also necessary spiritual practice.

As a reminder, consider this description as a way to understand what I mean by alert yet relaxed awareness. When we are in nature and observing a beautiful scene, such as the sunlight on the ocean, or the radiant leaves of autumn lighting up a mountainside, or a breathtaking sunset across a field of mid-summer wheat, we are alert and awake. We are fully present. We are not alert in the sense of being stressed and waiting for something bad to happen. We are in the moment, aware and observing. That is the kind of alert yet relaxed presence you are aiming for in meditation.

Also, bear in mind that this process goes in stages. You may spend many weeks watching your thoughts after a meditation session. Then one day, you practice your Kriya techniques and there are no thoughts, and you experience a thought-free state. This may endure for a few days. Then another wave of thoughts intrudes on your meditation. Once more, you keep attention at your spiritual eye or crown — wait, watch and let them pass.

You may go many years, having peaceful thought-free meditations, then one day thoughts arise again with renewed force. You have simply hit another plateau that needs to be worked through. In the concluding chapter on Final Liberation verse 27 of *Patanjali's Yoga Sutras*, it is stated, "Even as one (an advanced practitioner) is naturally inclined towards spiritual freedom, breaks may occur due to thoughts directed towards objects. These are due to subliminal activators that are not yet dissolved." It is not abnormal to have breaks to the flow of thought-free awareness from time to time even as an advanced practitioner.

It must also be stated that the way to prevent re-accumulation of undigested thoughts, feelings and memories is to avoid situations, people or things that contribute to the problems. Patanjali also says, "Pain which is not yet experienced is to be avoided." Sage advice. When you can help it, do not put yourself in situations that will cause you hard-to-resolve mental/emotional anguish. Of course, sometimes life requires that we have to face such circumstances. In that case, do your best to resolve life's difficulties and practice having faith that whatever the outcome, you did all that you could. Then let it go and move on, giving it up to God or your chosen concept of divine consciousness.

Finally, you also need to practice learning to ignore your thoughts in light of higher contemplation. If your awareness is absorbed on contemplating your true nature, the divine, or your relationship to the wholeness of life, you are less likely to be disturbed by intruding thoughts. In this way, you can put your attention where you want it to go. Do you want to contemplate divine bliss and peace? Or does your mind want to process old memories? Let it. Then direct your attention to absorbing the concepts of divine bliss and peace until they become real to you. Experience and practice will help you learn a proper balance of when to watch thoughts and let them pass, and when to disregard them in favor of higher contemplation.

Trying Too Hard

Many spiritual seekers begin with great zeal and energy. They read *Autobiography of a Yogi* or any other work by an inspiring spiritual personality and try to immediately do and live exactly like that person. "If Yogananda could meditate for five hours without stopping, then I can too!" they may say. The seeker then endeavors to find a way to sit still, trying to meditate for an extended length of time, every day.

This may work. But usually, the enthusiasm only leads one to sit semi-conscious in a passive state for extended periods, thereby wasting their life and time. Or the seeker uses his or her will power, forces the issue and then burns out.

I suffered from this problem. In the beginning, I would meditate well for 20 to 30 minutes, but I was dedicated to my path and would force myself to sit for an hour or more. I would then either drift off into a daydream, convinced I was meditating, or I would force myself to sit up straight and stay awake for as long as I could, and consequently give myself a headache. I would be able to do this two or three times in a row, and then when I would come back to meditation after that, I was exhausted. I could not get the Kriya current to rise up the spine. It felt like I was trying to lift a weight twice my own body. I wondered, what was wrong with me? Was I not spiritual enough? Was I not good enough?

Finally, the next time I saw my teacher I broached the question. I said, "I'm trying to be a good yogi and meditate longer and deeper, but I always end up giving myself a headache or drifting off into revelry. What am I doing wrong?" His immediate response was, "Get more rest." He then told me to meditate for short periods of time, not overdoing it. He said that in time I would be able to sit for longer and deeper meditations, but so long as it was a strain or causing headaches, I needed to get more rest.

He explained that when we begin a serious exploration of our spiritual path, we are not only reorganizing and strengthening our nervous system, we are also strengthening and purifying the subtle levels of our consciousness. The body, however gross, is a manifestation of the totality of our consciousness. Our consciousness needs to rest between exercising it with powerful practices, such as Kriya Pranayama and Jyoti Mudra. This is no different from when we work out to strengthen our muscles and nervous system. We need to have periods of rest so those muscles and that nervous system can rebuild and handle a bigger load.

I do not want you to make the same mistakes I did. I want you to approach your Kriya and meditation practice in an intelligent, less forceful manner.

You need to pay attention to your current capacity. How long can you sit in meditation before you start to fall asleep, or daydream, or lose your ability to exist alert yet relaxed?

That is your current threshold. Make note of this. Then, when you are ready, begin to extend that period of time with a gentle use of your will. If you can sit for 30 minutes, then once a week aim for 35 or 40. When you notice you can do this easily every day, you have reached a new threshold.

This is also applied to the number of Kriya Pranayamas you practice. You may find that when you increase your Kriya Pranayama numbers, you may hit a point where it feels like you just can't do any more. For me, it feels like my body is fatigued and I can't lift the cool electrical current up through the spine very far. DO NOT CONTINUE TRYING IF YOU REACH THIS POINT. Back off. Try a mantra technique or simply sit in the silence. Or go take a nap, relax and rejuvenate, and then try again later.

It is easy to know when you have overworked your body. Your muscles ache, you feel fatigue, or you feel overwhelmed by small disturbances. Since you cannot see your energetic system or feel it in the same way, you have to watch for signs of fatigue. These include the feeling of trying to lift a heavy weight when you do your Kriya Practice. You may feel cranky or more easily irritable. Maybe you give yourself a headache when you practice. You might feel exceptionally tired or dull and inert. When this occurs, back off of your energetic meditation practices, and focus on simple breath awareness or mantra technique. Take more naps or get more sleep. Go for a quiet walk in nature. Letting your body, nervous system and energetic system rebuild and strengthen is just as important as consistently practicing Kriya Pranayama. Remember that.

Also, I typically advise to keep your attention in the spiritual eye center or crown center when meditating. Sometimes this, too, can feel difficult, and like you are straining to do it. Do not strain. Rest your awareness in your heart center instead. You can meditate well in the heart, and it is not as hard to do if you are not yet strong enough to hold your awareness easily in the crown or spiritual eye.

Bear in mind, the more mature you become in your practice, it will become effortless to hold your awareness in the spiritual eye during meditation or to release your consciousness through the crown chakra. It will be easy to meditate (effectively, not falling asleep or daydreaming and imagining you are meditating) for two to three hours at a time in a pure conscious state. This takes time, and you will know when you can do it effortlessly, because it will be enjoyable and effortless. In the meantime, do your best and then give yourself plenty of rest in between. This can be rest from intensive meditation, or even rest from physical activity.

Do not give up too easily, but be honest with yourself about when you really need a rest. Resting is excellent spiritual practice. As you fall asleep, hold the question, "What is aware of my body falling asleep?" Stay watchful. Even your time in between waking and sleep can assist your realization process. Also, regular exercise will strengthen your body, mind and nervous system. The healthier and stronger and more resilient your body, the easier it will be to stay alert yet relaxed while you explore the deeper aspects of your being through meditation.

Chapter Seven

THE FOUR GATEKEEPERS OF LIBERATION

"There are four gatekeepers at the entrance to the realm of Freedom (Moksha). They are self-control, spirit of inquiry, contentment and good company. The wise seeker should diligently cultivate the friendship of these, or at least one of them."
-Vasistha's Yoga II:11

Spiritual knowledge and profound states of consciousness are not simply the result of proper mechanical repetition of technique. Certain behaviors, mental states, environments and people can contribute to the acceleration of your soul's maturity. The *Yoga Sutras of Patanjali* is an excellent text to contemplate to gain insights into behaviors and procedures conducive to liberation of consciousness. Again, please see my commentary on the Yoga Sutras in the book *Kriya Yoga: Continuing the Lineage of Enlightenment* for more detailed information about the sutras.

The book *Vasistha's Yoga* is another text that provides appropriate guides and powerful supports for your spiritual maturation process. Specifically, Vasistha shares four ideas that he calls the four gatekeepers of liberation. They consist of practicing self-control, inquiry, contentment and surrounding one's self with good company.

Of self-control, Vasistha states, "The eternal is not attained by rites and rituals, by pilgrimage nor by wealth; it is to be attained only by the conquest of one's mind, by the cultivation of wisdom. Hence everyone — gods, demons, demigods or men should constantly seek the conquest of the mind and self-control which are the fruits of wisdom." He continues in the same verse, "He who even while hearing, touching, seeing, smelling and tasting what is regarded as pleasant and unpleasant, is neither elated nor depressed—he is self-controlled. He who looks upon all beings with equal vision, having brought under control the sensations of pleasure and pain, is self-controlled. He who, though living amongst all is unaffected by them, neither feels elated nor hates, even as one is during sleep—he is self-controlled."

Of inquiry he says, "They in whom the spirit of inquiry is ever awake illumine the world, enlighten all who come into contact with them, dispel ghosts created by an ignorant mind, and realize the falsity of sense pleasures and their objects." Vasistha then tells us how to practice inquiry in chapter two, verse 14 of his text: "What is inquiry? To inquire thus: 'Who am I? How has this evil of samsara (repetitive history) come into being?' is true inquiry. Knowledge of truth arises in oneself, and then there arises the supreme peace that passeth understanding and ending of all sorrow. (Vichara or inquiry is not reasoning or analysis: it is directly looking into oneself.)"

Vasistha says about contentment, "What is contentment? To renounce all craving for what is not obtained unsought and to be satisfied with what comes unsought, without being elated or depressed even by them — this is contentment. As long as one is not satisfied in the Self, he or she will be subjected to sorrow."

The final gatekeeper, good company, is described thus, "Good company enlarges one's intelligence, destroys one's ignorance and one's psychological distress. Whatever be the cost, however difficult it may be, whatever obstacles may stand in its way, good company should never be neglected. For good company alone is one's light on the path of life."

Vasistha summarizes his exposition on the four gatekeepers of liberation with these words, "These four — contentment, company of the wise, the spirit of inquiry, and self-control—are the four surest means by which they who are drowning in this ocean of samsara (repetitive history) can be saved. Contentment is the supreme gain. The wise are the best companions to the destination. The spirit of inquiry itself is the greatest wisdom. And, self-control is supreme happiness. If you are unable to resort to all these four, then practice one: by diligent practice of one of these, the others will also be found in you. The highest wisdom will seek you of its own accord."

Self-Control Explained

The practice of techniques done properly with attention and awareness begins the process of developing self-control. At first, you may have to train yourself to sit still for 15 to 20 minutes, focusing on your breath. You may not be completely focused on the breath. The mind may wander, but you will at least be sitting still in one place. This is excellent for beginning meditators and very necessary. Those who crave a spiritual experience, but cannot sit still or are impatient, will not get very close to their expectations, if at all.

Once you can sit still for your allotted time, then you begin the practice of gluing your attention to the chosen object of contemplation. In this example, the breath. It sounds too simple, and many say, "Yes, this is fine, but when will you show me the advanced techniques, that will really ignite my spiritual vision!?" Most meditators, even those who have been meditating for years or even decades, and those who have been initiated and taught the most powerful techniques, probably cannot hold their attention on the breath for 20 minutes without distraction. If you are an advanced meditator, try it and see. It may be you have been practicing correctly and developing your self-control these many years. If so, this exercise will be easy, and you will be one of the few who are successful. For those who notice difficulty in holding awareness only on the breath for 20 minutes, I would say, rather than seeking out advanced procedures and the highest masters, you would do well to use your time more efficiently and learn how to develop your self-control so you can hold your awareness on one simple object of contemplation for at least 20 minutes.

Why only 20 minutes? That is a long time to remain absolutely fixed in contemplation. If you can sit for that long in unbroken absorption, you can easily repeat that three, four, five, or even six times. Then you will see why I often say, the more complicated a meditation technique, the less advanced it is.

Self-control, when developed, accelerates your spiritual maturity in a number of ways. First, if you can hold your mind still on one object of contemplation, you have a better chance to regulate your states of consciousness at other times. Consider the idea of contentment. Contentment requires that you have the capacity to hold your attention on a state of satisfaction even in dissatisfying circumstances. It requires that you have the capacity to remain as fulfilled internally, while you experience an elating circumstance, as you were before the circumstance that you associate with elation.

Self-inquiry (Vichara) gives its fruits when you hold your awareness completely on the question in mind. When you are self-controlled, you ignore everything else and focus intently on the chosen line of inquiry. Why do some people get immediate internal responses when they inquire, "Who am I? What am I that experiences all of these different states?" Usually it is because that is all they are holding in awareness. They are not simultaneously thinking about a hundred other things. It takes self-control to ignore distractions. Remember, this is not to be daunting, only to explain that you might need to take time to develop your self-control. It is no different from any other skill you may have developed.

Distractions and lack of self-control are also one of the primary causes for failing in any endeavor. You may say you want to become a master violinist, yet you only spend one hour a day playing violin. The other five hours you have free, you spend playing the saxophone, guitar, mandolin and sitar. Your attention is not controlled. This may make you a good well-rounded musician, but it does not help your goal to become a master violinist. Similarly, you may say you want to build a successful business, yet you only spend two hours a day on business. The other eight hours of time you have allotted to your workday, you spend surfing the internet, on social media, daydreaming, walking your dog, etc.

The same can be said for your spiritual practice. Your experiences flow in the direction of your attention. If your attention is distracted or fragmented, so will be your experiences. If you can see, imagine, or call forth the divine light, awe and wonder in every experience, person, place or thing, your experiences are more likely to reflect that. I do not say 100% of the time, because there are other factors at play than our limited viewpoint as a personality. Yet, the direction of our attention is very important for the majority of our life experiences.

Keeping the company of the wise also requires self-control. The wise are typically drama free. They may not care to overthink things. They may avoid people, places or things that are forgetful of the light of Self-knowledge. If you want to keep their company, you need to be at peace with this.

This too requires self-control in the beginning. Why? Because most people are drunk on their karma and enjoy places, people or things that do not support the clear light of Self-knowledge. You may say, "If someone is so wise or enlightened, why can't they just see the best in me and accept me for who I am?" The wise person does do this. They see the best in you and accept you for who you are, but that does not mean they approve of your choices or behaviors that are not conducive to Self-knowledge. Their motivation, if they have one, is to kindle the flame of Self-knowledge into a steady sustainable blaze. If you insist on throwing water on the fire, they may ask you to leave and make room for someone else who has enough self-control to behave appropriately, even if that person, like you, might not fully understand why a certain behavior is required.

In your meditation practice, you will experience what you are able to contemplate with consistency. This is why in the Yoga Sutras of Patanjali, the limb of yoga known as meditation does not occur until after the capacities to internalize attention and concentrate are developed. Self-control is required for both of these. More will be said on this topic in the chapter on Contemplation.

Inquiry Explained

What are you curious about? Take some time over the next week to watch your thinking process throughout the day. Notice what you habitually wonder or mull over in your mind. There will be a pattern and consistency to it. That will give you a clear idea about your curiosity in this life. It may be a focus on God, on the negative or positive interactions you have in relationships, on how much you hate or love your job, music, adventure, health, etc. The subjects of your curiosity will often reflect what you are knowledgeable about or what you want to and often experience.

Personally, I have decided to be very careful about my language and thoughts. I noticed that the more I thought about or wondered curiously about a certain situation or circumstance, the more likely I would experience it. This was applicable to both good and bad situations.

Now, if I find myself having a conversation and saying, "Can you imagine what it must be like to go through that difficult circumstance?" I will immediately say to myself, "I don't really want to know. I was just making conversation." If I am with someone who does not understand the power of words, I will say it quietly to myself. Most people I spend time with are aware of the power of the curiosity of the mind and the power of words. In that case, I actually say out loud, "Truthfully I don't really want to know what it must be like to go through that experience." Then for the sake of balance, I wonder, "What would it be like if that person was experiencing a better, more uplifting situation? Now that would be interesting."

For the positive, when I am planning the future or considering certain experiences I would like to have in life, I use the same process. I sit still, get calm and clear and emphatically say to myself, "What would it be like to have that experience?" I imagine it with the same kind of attentive curiosity of a child. I do not hold a state of doubt and half-heartedly wonder. I really truly wonder, what WOULD that be like? Just as negative curiosity gives me the opportunity to find out, so does positive curiosity.

The idea I want to share is that by having self-control over your curiosity, you are more likely to experience what you are actively and one-pointedly curious about. This is equally applicable to your intensive meditative contemplation sessions.

As mentioned earlier in this text, Kriya meditation techniques help to prepare one's consciousness for proper inquiry. As we develop our meditative skills, it is easier for us to focus directly and completely on that which we want to know. The Kriya techniques, over time, allow us to hold our attention longer and longer on a mantra, or the breath, or the tranquility stillness that follows after practicing Kriya Pranayama. This capacity can then be directed towards contemplation.

Now instead of locking our attention in a state of stillness, we can bring up curious questions, such as:

"What am I in relationship to this wholeness of life?"

"What IS the point of all these repetitive experiences?"

"Is God real? If so, then what is God really?"

"What am I?"

"What is that witnessing consciousness that experienced my dreams last night, my meditation this morning, my conversation with my friend, my ride to work, etc.?"

We can focus on these questions, letting them rest in our spacious alert-relaxed awareness, until the answers dawn. How rapidly or clearly these answers dawn depends on how well we have developed the skills through our meditation techniques to concentrate and observe in a relaxed-alert manner.

What is a relaxed-alert manner? Remember a time when you were observing something with curiosity. You were not thinking about it, you were only waiting to see what happened. Typically, you are in this state when you are sincerely interested in the outcome of a situation, or the answer to a question. This is an important point. Your topics of contemplation need to be based on your own genuine curiosity, and not because I or any other perceived authority figure told you, "You should contemplate a certain theme."

Contemplate your own genuine spiritual questions. The examples given above are what draws my attention. No matter what questions you have, there is a natural spiritual joy and value in practicing inquiry. No matter what you inquire into, in time you will have all your questions answered and you will run out of questions. Then all you will be able to do is rest in your own Self. Hence, at peace. You will then be personally knowledgeable and at peace. To this end, I sometimes like to inquire, "What would it be like if I had zero need to have my questions answered?"

We can also get directly to the point of inquiry by remembering Ramana Maharshi's approach. When a seeker would approach Ramana and pose a question, the question rarely mattered. Ramana would always direct the seeker back to his or her Self. To many questions he would appropriately respond, "Who is asking the question? Find that out." He would direct the seeker to focus on the who in "Who is asking the question?" rather than the proposed question.

Why would this be so effective? Because the ultimate source of satisfaction and peace resides in "knowing" and "being" one's Self. All other questions are just sublimations of this one ultimate difficulty. That is the difficulty of "knowing" and "being" one's Self. Why do we ask questions? Because we are disturbed in some way. This can be overt or subtle. When we are content and resting in a clear space, we have no questions.

Questions indicate a need to have something satisfied. We usually ask questions when we are disturbed by doubt or uncertainty. What is the danger with questions? It is that there can always be more questions. The universe is infinite and the mind wants to understand it all. Yet the mind cannot. In an infinite universe, there is no end to what can be questioned. When we are identified with the mind, we keep seeking, and asking, craving more satisfaction through having our concepts, experiences or ideas validated.

Maybe you know someone who, rather than sitting down quietly to meditate and breathe, always has just one more question they need answered before they can meditate effectively. Sometimes the solution to clearing doubts is not to continue to pursue one's doubts, but to take one's attention away from one's doubts for a while. Maybe the solution is to find out, "Who has the doubts?"

If we can focus on "who" needs the questions answered, we will then realize what we are, and that we are the infinite consciousness. When you are the infinite consciousness, you don't have to ask about it anymore. You no longer require validation for your ideals, ideas or experiences because you see and experience everything as it is — whole, infinite, flowing through countless perspectives of perception in this ever-changing world of form.

Please keep all of this in context. Questions can be very helpful as we interact in the world through our role-ego-personality. They help us understand the world of activity and form. When your car breaks down, you ask your mechanic to fix it. That makes sense. When you want to have a good relationship, you go to a counselor and ask how that can be realized. In the world of form and activity, there are appropriate recipes for success in every endeavor. If you want to know how to calm your mind, it can be helpful to ask a spiritual teacher who has calmed her mind how it is done.

When it comes to understanding perceived spiritual realizations, the mind can only take us so far. You cannot *think* your way into spiritual understanding or clarity. Although thinking can help, you plan your approach to realization. Inquiry is not thinking in the usual sense. Essentially, it is like a prayer or intention that is calling a direct experience to you. When you realize something through inquiry, it is not going to reveal itself as a series of thoughts in paragraph form. It will dawn as a direct immediate experience.

Once you have the direct realization of the "who" who is asking all the questions, you will not be able to describe it in words. Yet, when you meet another person who has also had the same experience, they will understand you. They will also not need you to talk about it, because they too can only "know" and "be" it. Talking and words require concepts and the mind. Direct experience cannot be contained with concepts. You suffer because you identify with the mind, rather than the whole you.

Once you start experiencing the direct realizations of inquiry, you will then see that thinking and the mind are only one small aspect of a vast infinite intelligence of which you are a part. You will then be less concerned about figuring spiritual things out through thinking or equations. You will understand directly the truth of that which you want to know. You will be quiet and content.

Contentment Explained

Why do we seek satisfaction in any form? Because we are not content with what is immediately present. This applies to mundane and spiritual cravings. As we know, many come to the spiritual path because they are craving a different experience. By attending to spiritual practices, we hope and desire that all our problems will be resolved. By having the ecstatic vision of a divine being, we believe we will be free and fully liberated from sorrow. We then hinge our happiness on our spiritual practice like an addict lusts for his chemical fix. If you take some time to consider the psychology of an addict in relationship to his addiction, you will see that many spiritual seekers demonstrate the same psychology, except in a more socially acceptable fashion.

Yet still, the craving of the addict and the craving of the seeker are the same. The seeker feels she cannot be happy unless she meditates or prays. She feels her life is lacking if she cannot visit her guru. She will not make it into heaven if she does not read her scriptures or recite her mantra the appropriate number of times. All these reasons contribute to unhappiness. These are all reasons the mind gives to rob her of the contentment that is ever present, right now.

This is not to say one should not meditate, pray, chant or commune with a guru. I have described why these practices are most definitely important. One of my criticisms of the modern non-dualism movement, which often focuses on contentment exclusively, is the lack of disciplined training to realize non-dualism. When your mind and nervous system are out of control, it is much harder to know your Self. This is probably why most non-dualist teachers are very good at talking people in circles rather than helping their followers map out a path to actually experience the Self.

Self-realization is attained through a balanced approach of surrender/contentment and proper training. Contentment without training will leave one floating in unconscious delusion. Training without surrender will leave one stuck in a loop of spiritual ambition. Time-tested meditation practices and inquiry, combined with surrender/contentment, reveals the reality of delusion and allows one to become conscious of one's own role in the creation of this delusion.

Instead of sitting passively in a moment that is full of pain or suffering and simply "being here now," we can consciously consider our role in this pain and adjust our circumstances as best we can. The disciplines and techniques of yoga assist in arranging our inner and outer life situation such that we are able to deal with difficulties as they arise and avoid future difficulties in a state of contentment. It is one thing to hear a spiritual teacher say, "Don't worry about it. It's all God or Self," when the roof is caving in. Yet that does not help you if you have not been able to realize that fully and completely through your own personal practice and exploration. I say this to encourage you to focus on your spiritual practices and explorations, rather than be sucked into the false idea that all we need to do is be content in the now. Learning to master one's consciousness while developing contentment is an ideal approach in this era.

In relationship to our spiritual work, the practice of contentment calls us to surrender the present moment at all times, even if we missed a meditation or prayer session. There is no spiritual value in holding thoughts of discontent in one's mind if we sometimes miss or avoid a spiritual session. So long as you are relatively consistent with your meditation and

Self-inquiry practices, there is more value in being content at all times, than there is in holding any thoughts about how you have failed in the past.

Spiritual techniques and practices that help to develop contentment are for intensive periods of personal training. This is similar to exercising your body. You do not exercise all the time. You exercise on a regular schedule, so you can live your life fully. If you miss an exercise session, chances are you are still going to be as strong the next time you work out. As long as you are consistent, there is no need to be concerned about those times when a session is missed due to life events getting in the way. The same can be said for spiritual practice.

Can you really live your life fully if you are always thinking about spiritual practice? No. You can live your life fully if you do your best to be regular with your personal spiritual training sessions, your daily meditation practices. At other times allow yourself contentment and call forth the experience of wholeness to permeate every moment. Then if you fail to be as perfectly spiritual as your expectations would like, it will not matter. You will be existing in the final state of liberation anyway, that of contentment. In this regard, your every moment becomes a spiritual practice. Isn't that why you are practicing meditation in the first place, to finally rest content in Self-realization?

The spiritual practice of contentment itself is extolled throughout time. Many realized yoga teachers have stated that for practice to give its full effects, one must meditate and attend to spiritual work without expectation of results. That means that every time you sit to meditate or engage a spiritual method, you do so without concern about what will happen next. If the mind becomes calm from the practice, that is fine. If the mind does not, that is fine. If an ecstatic vision of the

Goddess Kali comes to you, that is fine. If you are only aware of the space within the room and sensation of your breath, that is fine.

When you practice in this way, you are truly and completely honoring and acknowledging the full divine presence as it is. Be cautious of saying, "God, I will recognize you in a blinding light, but not in the gentle movement of the breeze against my cheek." When you accept the divine infinite consciousness for all that it is, you acknowledge, "Self of all, you are the divine ecstasy that comes from time to time, and yet I also know you are the pain in my back, my obsessive thoughts about work, and the flowing curtains that flutter over the open window in this meditation room." When our experience of Self becomes so vast to include all experiences, it is easy to understand the value of contentment against the alternative.

We know that EVERYTHING is God or Divine Spirit. The sages throughout the ages have proclaimed this to be true. Yet, those with limited vision ignore this and say, "God is joy and light and love. When I feel these things, then I will know I am with God." If we pay attention to the sages, we would know that, yes, God is joy, light and love. He is also pain, darkness and hatred. Spirit is Everything. It does not exclude anything. To the sage, which you are becoming through these processes, there is no preference given to joy, suffering, light, darkness, love, hatred or neutrality. They are all experiences of the divine wonder and awe of the Self.

The methods and practices outlined in this work clarify your consciousness and reveal the knowledge of Self you seek. Their effects are similar to regular exercise or taking a vitamin supplement to improve health. We do not experience the capacity to run for 10 miles with no rest after our first jog. Imagine how ridiculous it would look if someone cried and complained that they could not run a marathon after a few weeks of training. So long as they trained appropriately every day, they would eventually be able to run the marathon. The same is true with our spiritual work. The main difference is that a marathon has a set definition of distance to be run. This distance is the same for everyone.

In our spiritual practices, the effort and work is personal. This means there is no set mathematical gauge provided by the outer world to validate our progress. Ultimately, this implies we will not know when we have completed our spiritual work until it is done. When we are discontent, we will constantly question, "Is this enough? Have I done enough? How much more do I have to do?" If we can take on the mantle of contentment in relationship to our spiritual work, we will not ask these questions. We will practice with love and devotion until the task is complete. Then the task itself becomes inspired. We realize the task itself is not about reaching an end. It is about realizing every breath, every interaction, every dream, every bauble, every failure and every success as a ripple in our infinite timeless consciousness.

In the Yoga Sutras it is stated, "When one is content, there arises unexcelled happiness." As I have written in another book, *A Course in Tranquility*, when we are happy for no reason, then no reason can take our happiness away. If there is a goal to contentment, it is to allow us to experience happiness, regardless of any circumstance or situation. It is possible. It becomes easier the closer we come to realizing our Self. Our Self is realized through personal mastery and direct experience of what is true, which arises through consistent meditative exercises and intelligent application of contemplative Self-inquiry. Contentment is realized through practice.

Discontentment is due to our belief and conditioning that our happiness depends on external situations. To practice contentment may take hard work in the beginning. We may be so used to being discontented with ourselves, with what happens and the people around us, that it feels like a Herculean task to take up contentment. Yet it is necessary. It requires vigilance of our awareness to notice when we slip into a mood or state of discontent. Then it requires will to decide to create a feeling of contentment no matter what is happening in our present moment. Meditation increases our capacity for maintaining awareness. It also increases our capacity to use our will.

Beginning meditators must use their will power to stick to a disciplined practice. Each successful session increases one's capacity to use will power to sit in meditation. In time, the meditator will sit to meditate on schedule despite any feelings or thoughts or doubts that would've prevented the session during the novice stage.

Once the meditation routine is stable and undisturbed in its consistency, the Kriya Yogi can then direct her attention to applying that same disciplined awareness in everyday experiences. She can go to work, talk to her friends, enjoy a hike, all the while remaining aware of the fluctuations in her consciousness, which will be revealed as random thoughts, feelings and experiences.

As the capacity to live one's life while remaining as the internalized observer grows stronger, the next step is to detach one's sense of contentment from the experiences, emotions and thoughts that arise throughout the day. Her practice then includes holding to a state of contentment and peace no matter what arises and falls in her internal or external experience. The difficulties that arose as she first trained herself to sit still in meditation, and then to remain vigilant as the observer of her internal and external experiences, will be the same. Since she has had success in these previous endeavors, she now knows what will be required of her to call forth and maintain a state of contentment in all circumstances.

The trials and mental obstacles will be particular to her personality. There is no general recipe that can be given on how to develop the capacity to remain aware of the changes that occur in one's consciousness and how to use one's will power towards Self-mastery. The techniques provided in this text are a foundation for the process, but each of us must pay attention to our own way of learning and follow that inner guidance that arises through grace AND trial and error.

This can be compared to a person first riding a bicycle. You can tell someone the basic idea about how to ride. Build up momentum to help keep the bicycle upright. Then put your foot on the pedals and start pedaling to keep yourself moving forward. Don't make any quick turns until you feel comfortable riding in the forward direction., etc. Yet, what is the reality of learning to ride a bicycle? You learn by doing. The initial instruction is helpful. It is the combination of this instruction, crashing, getting back up and trying again, until you have the "aha" moment of how it works. It cannot be broken down into a recipe. Eventually, the nervous system and muscles simply catch on. This is also how you learn to develop contentment as you practice Kriya Yoga Vichara and throughout your life experiences.

As you work to develop your capacity for contentment, remember the words of Vasistha, "There is no power greater than right action in the present. Hence one should take recourse to self-effort, grinding one's teeth, and one should overcome evil by good and fate by present effort... One who says 'fate is directing me to do this' is brainless, and the goddess of fortune abandons him. Hence, by self-effort acquire wisdom and then realize that this self-effort is not without its own end, in the direct realization of truth."

Good Company Explained

The company you keep is a reflection of your inner state of consciousness. We return to the dream analogy. When dreaming, EVERYONE in your dream is a creation of your own consciousness. When you experience a violent person, a sad person, a happy person in a dream, it is only ever and always you. You can tell a great deal about your consciousness by the types of people you spend time with and how these people typically make you feel. The feelings you have in relationship to the people you surround yourself with are only a reflection of your inner world. The people themselves are mirrors. When you can finally accept this, make peace with this and live your life in this way, you are much closer to full Self-realization.

This analogy is often difficult to accept. Why? Because it is easier to blame something outside of our selves for a negative event then it is to take responsibility that it was our own inner conditioning that precipitated the event. The same is true for positive events. Isn't it usually much easier for a person to think a guru, savior or divine being is the result of good fortune or experiences that feel like an elevation of consciousness? The fact remains that we could not experience a contented event or elevation of consciousness if we did not already have that capacity within us. The external person or situation is only a reflection of our inner states.

Knowing this, we can approach the clarification of our consciousness by both attending to our inner state and the outer state. The inner work is accomplished through our Kriya meditation practices, Self-inquiry (Vichara) and the development of contentment. The outer work is accomplished by doing our best to surround ourselves with the people and situations that contribute to our goal of Self-realization.

Be aware of this dynamic in relationship to the company you keep. Many people enjoy their moods or scattered states of consciousness. If you are maintaining a consciousness of peace and clarity, you may find yourself challenged by others. If you maintain your clarity in spite of this, the other party may leave you alone. This can seem painful if you value the friendship, and it can make one feel lonely. However, it is important to remember that clarity and peace are more beneficial on the spiritual path than resonating in a state of anxiety, anger, drama or consistent frustration, just to make friends feel comfortable. If you choose peace and clarity, and they do not want to, that is their prerogative, and it is best to let them go. In time, with patience, you will attract those who are also seeking to resonate in clarity.

You can also seek out others who are relatively drama free, peaceful and Self-knowing. If your inner consciousness is still resonating in discontent, this may be challenging for you. However, that is a good sign. When you are with one who is content and Self-knowing, any frustrations, feelings or thoughts that arise in their presence give you a clear indication of what you need to work out internally to also experience peace and Self-knowing.

You may also find that as you approach content and Self-knowing people, they may not appear to want to spend much time with you, particularly if you are often in a state of psychological turmoil. Rather than take that as an affront, spend some time contemplating what internal changes are required to share their same frequency. If the person is open to your questions, maybe ask them directly what could be required to spend time with them. As long as you are sincere, a content Self-knowing individual will speak directly to you about this.

The reason many real "holy people" seem cold and aloof, when approached by "devotees," is because many seekers do not really wish to know what may be required of them to realize the Self, and are only seeking validation for their own misguided understanding. Remember, the person you see as a "holy person" outside of you is only a mirror of your inner states. If the "holy person" doesn't entertain your presence or questions, that is a reflection of your own inner capacity to benefit from the archetype of holiness and Self-knowledge within you.

This is a good time to consider what good company actually is. Many in our current spiritual culture consider a holy person to be pious, always kind, dressed in white robes and always spouting wise platitudes. I have found there are plenty of people who can pretend to play this role, based on these expectations, who have no real inner realization. In my experience, the person of good company is one who is internally at peace with their unique role in this world. The person knows what they are, beyond name or form. They may speak with kind or harsh words. Their actions may seem good and holy, or they may seem crude and wordly. Their actions may even be a combination of what we typically judge to be good and bad. Beyond their actions and words, they will be authentic in their approach to life and will not pretend to be anything other than what they are. According to Vasishta, they "will live a natural and spontaneous life, contentedly."

These are the people of good company. If they are interested in spiritual practices, they will be a good and authentic guide. However, not all will have the inspiration to play the role of a wise teacher. Yet by being in their presence, and living authentically as they do, you will still be moved by the proximity of their consciousness to deeper Self-realization.

Take time, on a daily basis, to contemplate and apply at least one of these four gatekeepers of liberation. The more often you reflect on their necessity for your Self-realization, the greater the likelihood that you will be inspired to cultivate them in your everyday life.

Chapter Eight

CONTEMPLATIVE PRACTICES

The crown jewel of Kriya Yoga Vichara is the capacity to know and to be. To know what you are, beyond name and form, to know that you are also the ever-changing phenomena of nature, to know that you are the very capacity for perception and experience in any realm, is divine knowledge. To live and exist at peace as this timeless knowledge is divine being. Kriya Yoga techniques prepare you for this realization by purifying, strengthening and aligning your physical, mental and astral consciousness so that it may clearly perceive what is real. Vichara is the method of contemplation that provides direct insight, knowledge and experience into what is real. Your consciousness must be properly tilled through the practice of Kriya, so that the seeds of Vichara can grow into the garden of Self-realization.

I often compare the inner work of Kriya Yoga Vichara to that of developing a healthy relationship. A relationship deepens and becomes richer as the years go by. This occurs because of your consistency, authenticity and integrity at cultivating the relationship. When you are inconsistent, scattered, undependable and disrespectful in a relationship, there is little chance that relationship will develop beyond a superficial frivolous waste of time. When you care deeply for the other person, take your time to listen and have heartfelt exchanges, and can support them upon their path, free of judgment, that relationship can turn into a healthy lifelong bond. Through that bond, you get to truly know the other person as well as yourself. Your spiritual practice follows the same blueprint.

To really know something requires consistent devotion, patience and curiosity. It is difficult to learn anything if one's attention is scattered, inconsistent or insincere. Through the practice of contemplation, we are directing our attention to that which we want to know and experience. This is fully supported by the Kriya Yoga techniques. It is through technique that we learn to master our attention. That way, if we are sincerely devoted to knowing what our relationship with God is, we can accomplish this with greater ease.

Once skillful in Kriya techniques, we now have the capacity to calm our mind, emotions and nervous system. We can direct our attention within and ask with devotion, "What is my relationship with God?" Through repeated attention to this question, while keeping our minds clear of any other distractions, the knowledge is called to us. Then we experience the knowledge directly. Should our awareness become distracted or scattered before the object of contemplation is realized, it is fine. We return our attention to the Kriya techniques to restore poise. Then we return to the question. This is the most efficient way to have your spiritual questions answered.

Final spiritual realization is often falsely characterized as an obliteration or annihilation of your present experience or capacity to experience. There an idea, that once Self-realized, everything will cease to exist. This is based on a tamasic view of life. When you long for this kind of realization, it is because you are not happy. Therefore, realization takes on the characteristic of a longed-for death after a life of great suffering. This is not what spiritual realization is at all.

When spiritually realized, you exist. While you exist, you know the true nature and reason for joy and suffering. You are not confined through definitions to a personality or state of consciousness. You can exist with the dregs of humanity, as well as with the clearest most sattvic being available. Or if you like, you can withdraw from all sense experience and exist free of any particular experience. In all circumstances, you know what you are, and you are aware of the necessity and value of all expressions of consciousness without judgment. In this way, you do not long for annihilation or escape from any circumstance. You may choose to remove yourself from a circumstance, but not because of attachment or aversion, simply because you are inspired to experience something else. This is because in time you have realized that all life and all experience (or non-experience) is eternal, infinite. There is no end to it. The Self-realized person loves all and sees everyone and everything as an expression of the Self, because she has had direct experience into the infinite eternal nature of consciousness.

How can you have direct cognition of this infinite eternal consciousness? How can you know the reason that there is both joy and suffering in the world? How can you see the most vile person (by your estimation) as the same divine consciousness as the hoary saint from majestic India? This occurs through effective contemplation and your capacity to cultivate a deep relationship with your Self. In this regard, by Self, I mean the whole you. This is the field in which your life experiences happen. It is the consciousness of which your mind, body, personality and history is only a tiny representation.

Contemplation can be practiced at any stage in your spiritual development. However, it must be attended to with attention, curiosity and patience. This means that if you are a novice meditator, your contemplation session needs to last as long as you can realistically hold your question in mind with curiosity. You do not want to turn your contemplative question into mechanical repetition. Nor do you want to act as if you are truly engaged in contemplation when you are actually only reciting the question to fend off distracting thoughts. As you become more skillful at your meditation techniques, you will be able to contemplate for greater lengths of time and thereby go deeper into the process.

Let us return to the relationship analogy. When you have a conversation with a dear friend, and you ask that friend a question, do you repeat that question over and over while the friend is considering a reply? No. You ask the question you sincerely want to know. Silence ensues as the friend considers the reply. You sit quietly, not thinking, not imagining what the person is going to say. You wait patiently, intently and curious about the response. You know your friend will speak because you trust her. So you are also relaxed. The answer is coming. You don't know when or even what it will be. If you already knew the answer, you wouldn't have asked! Finally, your friend speaks and now you have the answer.

Contemplation works in the same manner. After you have meditated, your system is calm, yet you are relaxed and fully awake. You sit in this silence, enjoying it for as long as you like. Then you begin your contemplative session. You already have a question in mind. You considered what you wanted to know before sitting to meditate. You ask the question silently, with feeling and intense curiosity.

"Why is there both joy and suffering in the world?"

Then you sit, waiting. You remain fully present in your body, abiding in the silence. You have shared your desire to have this question answered with the infinite consciousness of your "bigger" Self. As you wait, this consciousness is considering the best, most direct way to provide you with the realization you seek.

You may notice your attention wandering slightly. You ask the question again — not to be mechanical about it, simply to keep your attention settled on your intention to know. Maybe you even repeat two or three Kriya Pranayamas to reset your system and settle yourself back in the abiding silence. You maintain this process, for as long as you are able, or until the inner response is presented to you.

This kind of practice can give you direct and immediate realizations. Typically, the better you are at settling into silence after your Kriya techniques, the quicker realizations are presented. However, some answers may take weeks or months of contemplation until you are fully satisfied, feeling all that your need-to-know has been revealed to you. In these situations, you continue to contemplate a little every day on your chosen topic.

Some realizations will not be revealed in meditation, but in your daily life. The contemplative session has started the process, but maybe you can only have the answer revealed through an experience in your daily interactions. However the answers are revealed, we must remember that our life is a seamless whole. It is not divided into times we are meditating/contemplating and times we are not. This is why maintaining an alert, yet relaxed, content state of consciousness at all times is most important. Your spiritual questions can be answered at any time or any place. The contemplative practice session is ultimately only for you to be very clear and intentional about what you want to know. It is a request to access information from the totality of your being.

Ideally, you will have become skillful in calming your mind, emotions and nervous system before engaging in contemplation. This is important. Your witnessing consciousness observes all activity within your mind. You may have some curious unconscious questions you are not aware of. The witnessing consciousness will note that, and bring those answers to your awareness as well.

Imagine you are beginning a contemplation session before you have practiced Kriya meditation sufficiently to calm the mind. You begin to contemplate your chosen question, "What is my true relationship with Divinity?" Yet, in your mind, you are ruminating over the relationship drama your close friend has shared with you. Thoughts such as, "What would it be like to be in a relationship like that? How can he stand that kind of treatment?" are filling your mind. Although you are trying to contemplate a profound philosophical question, you are unconsciously contemplating a question related to relationship drama. The witnessing consciousness will take note, and may inspire your spouse to act out, thereby giving you the answer to the questions, "What would it be like to be in a relationship like that? How can he stand that kind of treatment?"

In time, you will become aware of how anything you contemplate, whether sitting quietly in meditation or on the car ride home from work, impacts your daily experiences. It is at this point that your Kriya Yoga Vichara practice consciously expands from sitting quietly twice a day, to Self-awareness and Self-mastery from moment to moment. Then life becomes quite interesting. You begin to realize you truly are never alone as the little personality you once thought you were. You realize you are constantly responding to and experiencing a living breathing relationship with your Self. It can be quite exhilarating.

The next chapter will provide helpful contemplative themes. Before considering what to contemplate, let us consider a useful meditation routine to create a solid foundation for contemplative practices.

Meditative Contemplation Process

Step 1: Determine your object of contemplation for this session. This can be a concept, a spiritual ideal or any philosophical question that deeply engages your interest.

Step 2: In your journal, write down the date and time and what you will be contemplating specifically. Be very clear on what you want to know.

Step 3: Practice and complete one of the meditation routines described previously in this text.

Step 4: Keeping your eyes closed, direct your attention to the space between and slightly above your eyebrows. Gently rest your attention here.

Step 5: Recall the object of contemplation you described in your journal. Bring it into your mind. If your contemplative theme is a question, ask the question with intensity and feeling. If it is a concept or ideal, think about all you currently know about this concept or ideal. Then ask, "What is the truth of this?"

Step 6: Rest quietly. Your attention is peacefully held between and slightly above your closed eyes. In your mind, you are aware of your curiosity to have your question answered. Yet you still sit quietly, patiently, as if waiting for a dear, old, wise friend to think over your query and provide the answer.

Step 7: If your attention wanders, ask the question again. This is not to force the process, nor is it to become a mechanical repetition like a mantra. This is only to redirect and refocus your attention on that which you want to know. Repeat as necessary, but make sure to leave space between each time you ask the question. It will be in the relaxed watchful silence that the answer arises in a flash.

Step 8: If the answer has been revealed, write down what you have learned in your journal. If it has not, sit a minute or two longer in the silence of meditation and conclude your practice. Repeat Steps 1 to 8 daily, until you are fully satisfied with the realizations that have been revealed to you.

It is important to note that certain themes of contemplation require action within your daily life. Remember that contemplation and Vichara are really about developing the capacity to have a relationship and conversation with your Self. Consider a friend seeking you out for advice to improve a certain life situation. If your friend asks you a question and you provide an accurate answer, yet that friend does not act on that advice, how many times will you repeat yourself? Will you eventually stop offering your wisdom when you see your friend only wants to talk, instead of take action to make improvements? While it is not useful to anthropomorphize consciousness, consciousness does work in a similar fashion. It is responsive to sincerity.

Through contemplation, when you are seeking knowledge, you are guided to the proper method of attaining that knowledge. Yet when you do not act on the guidance, the guidance will eventually cease to appear. Consider a meditation teacher who is approached by a student. The student asks, "My mind is so restless. How can I calm my mind?" The teacher responds, "Meditate on 'who or what' is able to experience this restlessness." The student returns time after time asking the same question. The teacher asks if the student has actually followed the instructions given. Each time the student responds in the negative. Eventually the teacher will save her breath for more responsive students.

It may be during your contemplative sessions that you have a direct inspiration in answer to your question. To fully act on what you have learned encourages your capacity to contemplate with greater clarity and accuracy. How is this so?

If you contemplate, "How can I experience Divine Love?" And your inner knowing reveals to you, that to experience Divine Love requires that you love all equally, both those you personally love, those you quite dislike and those you are indifferent towards. It is necessary to engage this in your daily life. You now know to experience Divine Love, you are to practice loving all equally.

Consider contemplating, "How can the infinite nature of consciousness reveal itself to me as it is, free of illusion and delusion?" Now imagine you have sat with this question in mind for many contemplative sessions. During your ninth session, you are inspired to open your eyes and look around. You see your everyday surroundings. Yet something in your heart is affirming that THIS is the infinite nature of consciousness, as it is, right now! If you can acknowledge this realization and endeavor to integrate it into your daily life, you may be surprised to experience that the infinite nature of consciousness does reveal itself to you, as it is, free of illusion and delusion, in nearly every moment.

If, on the other hand, you ignore this realization and instead say, "This can't be right. Where is the blinding light and the feeling that I've taken some fantastic drug? At least that is how all the yogis I've read about describe it!" Then you are affirming you don't really want to know the answer to the question you've posed and are only waiting for your preconceived notions to be validated.

Contemplation is a subtle practice. It requires patience, perceptive acuity to your inner states of being and a solid foundation in the basics of meditation. When inner knowing is revealed and you do your best to engage what you have learned in your daily life, you move closer to fully realizing that which you initially contemplated. You also have affirmed you are willing to participate in this subtle method of learning, and so your conscious capacity to experience knowledge directly through contemplation increases.

A word of caution should be shared at this point. If any of your contemplations lead you to the realization that you are special in any way, or have great spiritual wisdom and powers you need to share with the world, ignore this. If any of your contemplations lead you to the realization that it is acceptable to consciously engage in any harmful behaviors, ignore this. In the beginning, it can be difficult to decipher a higher realization from a personal fantasy. The healthier you are psychologically, the better. This is why I do not advise people to begin engaging in intensive yogic procedures unless they are as mentally, emotionally and physically healthy as they can be.

This is also why it can be helpful to have a realized, or at least skillful, mentor to assist the process. A mentor can help you avoid grandiose illusions mistaken for realizations. A mentor can help you see that all realizations are internal gifts that do not need to be validated. They are for you only. If they change the way you experience and live your life, this is fine. Your wisdom is your own.

As with all skills, contemplation improves through practice. Consider contemplation as you would learn a new language. In the beginning, you may only be able to ask simple questions. Sometimes you may even misinterpret the answers. With each success and mistake you make within the process of contemplation, you are gaining a better grasp of the language of consciousness. Your vocabulary grows over time. Some contemplative revelations may occur as an inner feeling. Others may appear as an image in your mind. Some revelations may appear through directing you to a book, or in a conversation with a friend. The greater your patience, trust and capacity to observe life happening around and within you, the more likely you will benefit through contemplative practices.

Chapter Nine

OBJECTS OF CONTEMPLATION

There are many diverse avenues of contemplation. Some people may contemplate the powers and presence of mythological gods and goddesses. Some may contemplate the nature of their mind. Some may simply sit watchful and alert observing all changes that rise and fall within and externally. Others may explore their burning spiritual or philosophical questions.

Your themes of contemplation will need to be something in which you are sincerely interested. If you are not interested in that which you are contemplating, you are less likely to have realizations revealed to you. This is why it is important to take up contemplation out of sincere interest, rather than because you believe it is good for you.

Now that you are skillful in meditation and know how to incorporate contemplation, consider the themes that follow to help encourage your practice. Choose one theme at a time. Continue your contemplative practices until you are satisfied with your realizations, or until you feel it is time to move on to another topic. Sometimes, we need to take a break from a specific theme of contemplation to give it time to mature in our consciousness.

Model your own personal themes after the questions, topics and scriptural quotes provided. Continue in your meditation and contemplative endeavors until all of your spiritually enlightening questions are answered. Then you will rest fully awake and at peace in your infinite eternal Self.

Spiritual and Philosophical Questions

Spiritual seekers may take up the path to enlightenment because they have deep philosophical or existential questions. The joy of contemplation lies in its capacity to give direct insights into those questions.

Humanity's deepest unhappiness comes from an inability to sincerely explore questions motivated by great suffering or confusion. When tragedy causes one to ask, "What is the point of this life, with all of this suffering?" Rather than sit, stewing in the grief, if we can turn within and earnestly ask this question, the profound truth of the matter may be revealed to us. This is not to invalidate grief. Grief and the process of grieving is a natural part of experiencing life as a human being. Yet, the questions that it may inspire can lead us to insightful realizations about our present sojourn in space-time.

As we wonder about the nature of God and reality, we may be inspired to contemplate. Too often people never investigate the nature of their beliefs and never outgrow dependence on fantastic ideas about what God or divinity is. (The fantasy pales by an infinite magnitude to the reality.) If we have doubts or confusion about the nature of divinity or reality, it is perfectly acceptable to create a theme of contemplation around these doubts.

Doubt is valuable to lead us to an exploration of truth. Doubt encourages us to find out what real faith is. That which is left after all our doubts are cleared will be the gem of faith, which is beyond any doubt. This does require an openness and trust to accept what we find as we explore our doubts. Sometimes we may have to face and accept aspects of our beliefs that we have held dear for many years or even lifetimes. Yet, if we can accept reality as it is revealed to us, due to our contemplative analysis inspired by our doubts, we may find a world alive with transpersonal truth.

Let the exploration of your beliefs guide you to that which will be of ultimate value in your contemplative processes. It will be the questions inspired by your interaction with the transient nature of your personal life experience that will reveal the gem of faith – living, breathing faith.

Let the following questions serve as an introduction to your contemplative practices, until you feel comfortable generating your own themes.

"Who am I?"

"What is the point of this life?"

"What is divine consciousness?"

"Why is there suffering in this world?"

"Why did I choose to live in this world that is a constant recurring cycle of pleasure and pain?'

"Is God really what I think he/she is?"

"What happens after we die?"

"What was I before I was born?"

"What does it mean to be spiritual?"

"Why am I afraid when I have no real reason to be?"

"What would it be like to live in the present moment?"

"What is my mind? Is it real?"

"Are we really one?"

"How can I be truly peaceful in this chaotic world?"

"How can I feel and acknowledge my infinite eternal connection with divine consciousness?"

"How can I live 'the good life'?"

"What is true spiritual love?"

"What am I?"

"Is this world experience real?"

Of all of these questions the most important is, "Who am I?" This was the foundation of Ramana Maharshi's work. It was his insight that if we could know completely and unapologetically "Who am I?" that all other questions would be irrelevant.

We ask all of our questions, because we do not know who or what we really are. When we have a spiritual or philosophical question that needs answered, we are unconsciously defining ourselves as a mind, personality and mental position. These things are necessary aspects of our being so that we may interact with the world of form, but they are not the totality of our being.

When Ramana Maharshi was asked about God, he would encourage the questioner to leave God alone and to find out "who" is asking the question. When asked about how to have more peace in this world, he would again encourage the questioner to find out "who" wants to have more peace in this world. This can seem maddening. It could even appear that the Maharshi was trying to avoid the questions, because he did not have an answer. Yet that will only appear so for those who do not understand the profundity of his direction.

Consider the natural world. Consider the magnitude of life on this small planet Earth. Consider the complexity, harmony and intelligence that must exist throughout this globe of rock and water for life to express as it does. In all of its intricacy and majesty, does life ask about God or suffering or divine consciousness? It does not, except in the human mind. Yet life continues to rise and fall in all its glory, beyond our capacity to fathom.

Consider your small self. Do you stop at the boundary of your skin? Are you not a part of a community or an ecosystem? Even if you're a hermit, you cannot exist separate from your environment. Has your mind, genetics and personality not been shaped by countless generations of ancestors? Has the culture in which you exist contributed anything to how you see and perceive the world? Does your physical nourishment ultimately come from a star (the Sun), which is also influenced by galactic phenomena, which in turn was produced by a universe?

This is superficially scratching the surface of the full import of what you would realize through the simple asking of the question, "Who am I?" This is why Ramana Maharshi would rather you realize and be "Who you are" rather than to chase the answer to questions that are miniscule in comparison. He also had the capacity to know that there can always be more questions after one is answered. However, to know who you are will ultimately put to rest all other questions.

This is not to say it is wrong to seek out answers to your personal questions. Why are we here if not to explore our unique interests as an individualized aspect of a holistic consciousness? Yet to remain true in your direct route to Self-realization, it is necessary to always keep in mind and return to the ultimate question of what you are, beyond any doubt, notion or concept.

It is easy to understand why more people might not sincerely want to know the answer to the question, "Who am I?" If you knew that, the game would be over. There would be nothing of interest left to explore. You would no longer have the capacity to play hide and seek with your Self through time and space. You would know where and what you are at all times. The mystery would be gone. The final score would be known before the sport had even begun.

Yet this is a fallacy created by our minds to obscure the full truth. It is like having an obsession with adventure novels rather than actually going on an adventure. It is like collecting indulgent recipes instead of actually preparing and serving those recipes. The awe and splendor of realizing your Self cannot be conceived of by a mind fixated in time, definitions and categories. This is why Self-realization cannot be described, proven or validated. It can only be experienced directly through methods laid out by others who have found a way to realize it.

To this end, no one can talk you into Self-realization. Nor can you talk others into it. No one can truly inspire you or carry you to Self-realization. Nor can you inspire or carry others. Everyone has his or her own inner drive. Others can reflect the inner calling, by showing up to mirror the circumstances and people necessary to make it possible. But we are drawn to Self-realization because of our own ripeness and preparedness for the process to complete itself. As it is a process, and we are all going through it. We can refer to the way of Self-realization made by others as a guide, but our final awakening will be an intensely personal experience.

Let your sincere questioning guide you to fulfill your own path to spiritual fulfillment.

Contemplating Images and Icons

Some spiritual aspirant's temperament may be better suited to contemplating an image or an icon. This is the path of bhakti or devotion in the traditional sense. It is still contemplation, because the end goal is to unite with, and thereby know, the reality of the divine image being worshipped.

All images of divine personalities (gods and goddesses) are representations of specific powers of consciousness. They are not separate entities, but aspects of the whole. If you can find and identify with one aspect of divine consciousness, you have found the whole. In the same way, if you find the hand of your lover, you have also found the rest of your lover's body.

This is why any type of devotion for the purpose of realizing a greater connection to the whole is valid. It will even apply to any person, place, thing, idea or activity. Why? Because there is nothing separate in this consciousness. Anything that can inspire devotion, if you can follow that devotion and let your mind be consumed by it, will result in Samadhi – cognitive absorption, the final limb of yoga as described in *Patanjali's Yoga Sutras*.

There is one trouble with devotional contemplation. Too often, a person becomes fixated on being able to experience an exulted spiritual state through the specific object or activity alone. They then become dependent on it.

Personally, I find it most effective to use devotional practices that require a specific object or activity to build up a positive flow of energy so that one can effectively practice Vichara, or Self-inquiry. Again, once you know what you are, beyond name or form, you can maintain that capacity for devotion towards all people, places and things.

Choose your icons of devotion based on your inner guidance and inspiration. Once you have generated a profound state of reverie, then proceed to your meditation and contemplation sessions. You may even ask the image of your devotion to help deepen and make clearer your spiritual practice.

Always keep in mind that the image of your devotion is an objectified aspect of your very Self, and not a separate entity. Contemplating that notion alone can encourage enlightening realizations.

Contemplating Enlightenment Texts

Spiritual texts are excellent sources in which to find contemplative themes. In fact, they were written to inspire contemplation. Contemplation of a sacred work begins in your silent meditation session. It grows and finally blooms into Self-realization through your consistent dedication to live with and patiently integrate the teachings the text contains.

The powers of a spiritual text are unlocked once you take the time to develop a relationship with it. This occurs through reading the work carefully, thinking about it throughout your day, trying to remember what you learned from it the night before, and then putting what you have learned into practice.

Do not be like one who collects spiritual literature so he can say he has read so many holy books. Take up one text at a time and make it a part of you. Let it change the structure of your consciousness to match the resonance of Self-realization. This may take months or years, and repeated reading and contemplation. It is worth it.

Over the course of my spiritual studies, there are only five books I have given most attention to reading. They are:

- *Autobiography of a Yogi*
- *The Bhagavad Gita*
- *The Yoga Sutras of Patanjali*
- *Talks with Ramana Maharshi*
- *Vasistha's Yoga*

Of these five, there are three I have read more times than I can count and I still continue to devote regular periods of contemplation to their exploration. If you ask me to comment on spiritual texts other than these three, I would not have much to say, because I have not devoted enough time to any other book. These texts are:

- *The Yoga Sutras of Patanjali*
- *Talks with Ramana Maharshi*
- *Vasistha's Yoga*

When I study one of these works, I focus specifically on that text alone. I do not read it to finish it. I read it to understand it. That may mean that I spend a week or more contemplating a sentence or two from the *Sutras of Patanjali* during meditation. It could mean that I reread two paragraphs in *Vasistha's Yoga* over the course of many nights before I fall asleep. Once I have a sense of understanding about what has been read, I move on to the next passage or sutra. This can take months or years to finish one book.

During my day, if I have a break or am going for a walk, I will try to remember what passage I was contemplating during meditation. I think about the principles and consider how I can apply them right now, in my active life. This saturates my mind and consciousness with the higher knowledge held within the texts I consider sacred.

This kind of work has a tendency to eliminate and crowd out any worry, anxiety or obsessive thoughts common to many people. If a mind is saturated with processing higher knowledge, it is less likely to respond to petty or troublesome mental habits. When the mind's resources are directed to this kind of contemplation, one's experience naturally reflects and validates the holistic vision of cosmic consciousness. Needless to say, contemplation of a sacred work that is dear to you can greatly accelerate your spiritual maturation process.

For general spiritual yogic development, consider reading my previous book *Kriya Yoga: Continuing the Lineage of Enlightenment* for a commentary on the *Yoga Sutras of Patanjali*. For the *Bhagavad Gita*, please see Roy Eugene Davis' book, *The Eternal Way*. Swami Venkatesananda's translation of *Vasistha's Yoga* is the best by my estimation. If you have a particular affinity for Paramahansa Yogananda, see his seminal work *Autobiography of a Yogi*. If you are drawn more to Ramana Maharshi, read the collected *Talks with Ramana Maharshi*.

I have found reading and deeply contemplating these works in the following order to be most beneficial.

- *Autobiography of a Yogi*
- *The Bhagavad Gita*
- *The Yoga Sutras of Patanjali*
- *Talks with Ramana Maharshi*
- *Vasistha's Yoga*

It may be that you resonate more with one of these works than with the others. Put more of your focus there. It may be there are other spiritual texts you find equally meaningful as those listed above are to me. Let those be a source of your contemplation. I share these five specific books because they have served as the foundation for this work called Kriya Yoga Vichara. Reading them can give you more meaningful insights into Kriya Yoga Vichara than it is possible to do is this one simple text you are currently reading.

However you proceed with your spiritual studies is up to you. My advice is to take your time. Integrate what you learn fully before moving on to something new. Let the process happen naturally within the boundaries of a disciplined schedule.

Below you will find a series of passages from *Vasistha's Yoga*. These are excerpts from my personal journal where I recorded thoughts after contemplating certain passages. Having a journal to chronicle your thoughts or realizations after contemplating a spiritual text can help permanently assimilate that which you have studied.

Follow the pattern in the text below in your own journal. Write out the sutra or paragraph you are contemplating. Then meditate and contemplate the meaning of the passage. Use the **Meditative Contemplative Process** described at the end of the last chapter. Finally, take time to write out your thoughts within your journal.

Your personal reflections can be as long or as short as you are inspired to write. Practice writing something down after each contemplative session. Let the examples below serve as a general guide for your own practice.

I.1 "Verily, birds are able to fly with their two wings: even so both work and knowledge together lead to the supreme goal of liberation. Not indeed works alone nor indeed knowledge alone can lead to liberation: but both of them together form the means to liberation."

Liberation of consciousness, also known as enlightenment, is the essence of our being. To be liberated is to be free. Enlightenment is complete freedom from all limitations. Once the knowledge of being free arises, we can then act from that knowledge. Actions are then free from compulsion and aversion, and are synergistically supportive of Self-knowledge.

Knowledge of one's Self as an unconditioned limitless being provides proper perspective in relating to the temporary conditions of human existence. When the confusion arises that the passing experiences in life are the total truth of what we are, ignorance is in effect. Living from a state of Self-knowledge, there is no need to cling or act irrationally. Life then proceeds freely and without strain, making all experiences more enjoyable because all experiences are then in proper perspective to our true Self.

No matter the state in which we find ourself, as long as it is conditioned in some manner, this indicates a cause for the condition. Causes are the energies that empower present experiences. We may not always know the exact reason our consciousness is conditioned in a certain way, but having the knowledge that attachment to the condition enforces the condition, we can then choose to release the attachment. Then the conditioning is no longer supported and is allowed to exhaust its energy and thereby dissolve.

Action that is performed while centered in Self-knowledge is the work that provides the means to liberation. All other action is binding and limiting. When a person acts out of desire or compulsion, that desire becomes stronger due to reinforcement. When a person acts out of fear or aversion, the aversion is further strengthened. In both instances, conditioning and limitation grow. Centered in Self-knowledge, any action is performed in neutrality, neither out of desire or fear.

Abandoning living the life created through our past actions in favor of practices that promote Self-knowledge is often a misguided attempt to escape the life we have created. Needing to escape a situation implies aversion to that situation, and further indicates lack of Self-knowledge. A balanced approach of interacting with the circumstances of life, while also giving priority to developing Self-knowledge, is the means to liberation of consciousness. Then Self-knowledge is stable to express no matter the conditions in which we find ourselves. Liberated souls live in this way.

To act in the world is to function in duality, the constant flux of opposites: pleasure, pain, light, dark, happy, sad, detached, attached, action and inaction. Enlightenment is both beyond and encompassing of the duality. A fully liberated person is not concerned with these opposites and experiences them as they occur, seeing them as a temporary manifestation of one wholly integrated reality. Liberated people know the truth of what they are beyond conditioning, and act from that realization, allowing circumstances to be what they are while acting appropriately, free of compulsion or aversion. Utilizing both our wings, knowledge of what we are at the core of our being and work (freely performed actions) in the world, allows us to live as enlightened people do, and actualize our complete liberation of consciousness.

I.3 "This world appearance is a confusion, even as the blueness of the sky is an optical illusion. I think it is better not to let the mind dwell on it, but to ignore it."

The world appearance (life situations, experiences) appears to be real (important, meaningful) but is really only confusion in the mind of the observer, much like the blueness of the sky. The sky itself is not blue. The blueness occurs from the white light of the sun being scattered into blue light by molecules in the atmosphere. The sky itself remains colorless and infinite despite this effect of light. When our consciousness is not scattered by the mind into the thoughts that veil reality, the world appearance can be known for what it is, a condensed wave of consciousness in an infinite sea of consciousness. By not dwelling on the world appearance and "ignoring" it, the tendency to mistake the world appearance for reality decreases. Then the true nature of reality is more likely to be perceived.

Giving attention to the experiences of life through compulsive thought or obsessive analysis strengthens the inclination to identify one's being with a false sense of Self. The Self of everyone is not affected by life experiences. The Self of everyone is the consciousness that supports the existence and perception of life experiences. The word "ignore," as used in this verse, does not mean to refrain from noticing the world appearance with the senses. While embodied, observation through the senses is natural. To "ignore" the world appearance is to refrain from investing energy into identifying one's Self with what one experiences.

The purpose of spiritual practices, such as meditation, prayer, mantra, ritual, etc., is to train the mind to become focused on a concentrated point. Through concentration, one is able to detach from average clouded states of awareness and thereby "ignore" the world appearance. The mind is not then able to haphazardly identify with every passing experience, be it a situation, a thought, or an emotion. In time, one learns to effortlessly maintain this focused awareness while not engaged in specific mental exercises. When this occurs, one's path of Self-realization can become intensive. The very aspect of being alive becomes an all-encompassing spiritual practice. The one consciousness that supports the world appearance is then clearly perceived as the Self of all things and confusion is replaced by Self-knowledge.

I.29 "Indulgence in sense-pleasure poisons the mind in such a way that its effects last several lifetimes. Only one of Self-knowledge is free from this."

Life is habitual. The habits one entertains directs how one's life develops. When consciousness is directed to fulfilling the pleasures of the senses, the habit of looking for fulfillment in the world gains strength. As momentum builds in this direction, one moves further from the truth that lasting fulfillment is found while centered in the Self. In time, the search for fulfillment in the world becomes so all consuming, that one's intelligence becomes perverted and rarely does the realization arise that the search for peace in the world is actually taking one further away from the only "place" peace is found.

All souls have the right to three things: being, consciousness and bliss. In fact, being, consciousness and bliss is the very essence of the soul as an individualized unit of pure consciousness. It is the actualization of being, consciousness and bliss together that is the only lasting fulfillment one can experience. All striving and seeking, for whatever reason, is motivated by the impulse to experience these three characteristics.

When the soul mistakenly identifies with the mind, which is an instrument of the soul for relating to the material world, thoughts begin to arise that state, "fulfillment can only be found in objects of the material world," thereby creating confusion. The soul can perceive the mind, but the mind cannot perceive the soul. To correct this confusion one simply needs to develop Self-knowledge, which results from shifting one's perspective from identification with the mind to identification with the soul.

When identified with the mind, thoughts or emotions may ceaselessly flow through one's awareness, seemingly beyond one's control to regulate. When identified with the soul, stillness and serenity in the present moment are the predominate experience. To shift perspective from the mind to the soul, one can acknowledge thoughts by watching them pass with detachment, as if watching a river flow while simultaneously imagining what it would feel like to be peaceful, no matter what is observed in one's awareness.

With practice, thoughts become less influential and less stressful. The ability to make the shift to soul awareness becomes easier as identification of the Self with the mind weakens. Then one will habitually function from the perspective of the Self, and be able to live in Self-knowledge. Stable in Self-knowledge, the alternating waves of 'desire for gaining' and 'aversion to losing' an object or experience of the senses no longer disturbs one's consciousness. Once centered in the Self, one already embodies the essence of what would otherwise be sought in the world. Being consciousness-bliss without the necessity of any external condition to bring about the experience is then natural.

II.1 "This diversity arises on account of mental modifications and it will cease when they cease."

Categorization of the world into concepts, such as "this is," "this is not," "I," and "you" are the result of mental conditioning. The distinction between the subject one is believed to be and the objects one perceives, is purely mental. For the sake of verbal communication such ideas have arisen. Diversity and separateness in the world is not real. Much like one can be confused by imagined identification with thoughts, one may also experience confusion by imagining the structure of language, which by its very nature divides and categorizes, to be the reality. Rather, realize language as a vehicle for communication between two points of view within the one wholly unified infinite consciousness. The experience of diversity within the infinite consciousness ceases when thoughts that support the belief that one is isolated cease. This requires reflecting on one's identification with a particular point of view, or ego-sense, and releasing attachment to it. Maintaining notions of whom or what one is creates a veil preventing one from experiencing reality as it is, which is unlimited and free. Dedication to entertaining thoughts that support a specified expression of personality in consciousness creates the feeling of isolation. One then acts as if cut off from the source of being. This then provides the opportunity for one to act inappropriately in the world.

Reality is always what it is. Nothing can change that. However, by identification with thought and ego-sense a person can act in a way that has no bearing on reality. If a person has a mental disorder that causes them to hallucinate and perceive what is not real, the person will act in such a way that, although it seems perfectly natural to them due to complete absorption in the hallucination, it seems crazy to an observer not suffering from the hallucination. Living through the identification with thoughts and ego-sense is, in a sense, like living fully absorbed in a hallucination.

The ending of mental modification can be experienced directly in two ways. The first way is to stop giving attention to thoughts that divide the world into subject and object relationships. The second requires inquiring into what one is at the core of being. Both of these methods can be practiced together intensively. When engaged and active in the world, thoughts that make a distinction between a subject and object can be noted and then released. At times when an opportunity for inner contemplation arises, one can observe their awareness and inquire into what one is beyond all modification of thought and conditioning.

II.3 "Countless have been the universes that have come into being and dissolved. In fact even the countless universes that exist at this moment are impossible to conceive of. All this can immediately be realized in one's own heart, for these universes are the creation of the desire that arises in the heart like castles built in the air. The living being conjures up this world in his heart and while he is alive he strengthens this illusion; when he passes away he conjures up the world beyond and experiences it- thus there arises worlds within worlds just as there are layers within layers of a plantain stem. Neither the worlds of matter, nor the modes of creation are truly real; yet the living and the dead think and feel they are real. Ignorance of this truth keeps up appearances."

The universe and all experiences within it are sustained by the intentions and desires created through the thoughts of living beings. Pure consciousness is the heart of every being. By returning attention to pure consciousness, one can realize the source of creation and the root causes of experiences within creation. By identifying with one's pure conscious nature, rather than the personality and external circumstances in life, Self-mastery is possible.

Knowing that experiences are the results of thought patterns enables one to come to terms with the causes of present circumstances and to thereby take responsibility for the future. Current experiences are the result of past intentions. Future experiences are the result of current intentions. The world one experiences, and the world one will experience in the future, can be directed through observation and regulation of thought patterns.

If one is not accepting of the fact that enlightenment is as natural as the wind blowing or the sun shining, one can observe the thought patterns that support that lack of acceptance and with gentle intention change the thought patterns. The essence of every person is whole, clear, serene and enlightened. When this is accepted as truth, one can then begin acting appropriately as an enlightened person.

II.4 "In this world, whatever is gained is gained only by self effort; where failure is encountered it is seen that there has been slackness in self effort. Self effort is of two categories: that of past births and that of this birth. The latter effectively counteracts the former. Fate is none other than the Self effort of a past incarnation. There is a constant conflict between the two in this incarnation; and that which is more powerful triumphs. There is no power greater than right action in the present."

All circumstances are the result of one's own desire to experience the circumstance. Once one's desire is firmly established, the results of that desire will manifest when the opportunity is ripe. Physical effort in the world is a means to expressing the effort that has already been made in the realm of desire, thereby providing proper conditions for the desire to bear fruit.

Circumstances that occur with seemingly little or no effort are the results of past self-effort. For example, one may be able to play a song on an instrument with ease due to past efforts in practice and performance, but when trying to play a song never heard before, the effort needed to play the new song may seem great without the same amount of past practice. Whatever one is presently capable or incapable of is the result of the degree of intensity of past self-effort.

Deep-seated desires and fears can direct the life of one who is ignorant of the fact that actions performed in the present are more powerful than past conditioning. To allow past desires and fears to dictate one's life maintains one's present experience. By accepting the capacity to change, and making an effort to acknowledge the causes of present experiences, one can adjust present desires and actions to reflect what is desired for a brighter future. Persisting in this way until results are satisfactory brings success.

Realizing one's enlightenment, as with all circumstances, is the result of self-effort made to this end. Nobody and nothing prevents the realization of enlightenment except the thoughts, beliefs and actions one makes that do not support this realization. Similarly, only one's own self-effort can assure enlightenment.

At the core of all people is an enlightened being, fully awake to the wholeness and serenity of pure consciousness. Rapid progress on the spiritual path is assured by coming to terms with past limitations, releasing them, and then making the effort to live like an enlightened being. The only difference between those who appear to be enlightened and those who do not is that those who appear to be enlightened have simply made the effort to live as they are at the core of their being. The enlightened ones are free of the dissonance created by not living in tune with their true nature.

II.13 "The eternal is not attained by rites and rituals, by pilgrimage nor by wealth; it is to be attained only by the conquest of one's mind; by the cultivation of wisdom. When the mind is at peace, pure, tranquil, free from delusion or hallucination, untangled and free from cravings, it does not long for anything nor does it reject anything. This is self control or conquest of mind and one of the four gate keepers to liberation."

According to the Yoga Sutras of Patanjali, "Yoga is the process of ending fluctuations and changes in the field of consciousness." Mastery of the mind is key to this process. Prayer, ritual, charity and pilgrimage are not the means by which enlightenment is realized. These actions may put one in a devotional mood, but if they do not calm one's mind, they are of no use towards enlightenment and serve the same function as any other action that promotes pleasant moods through entertainment. When the mind is under control, peaceful tranquility is the natural result and can be maintained voluntarily. A mind that is seemingly calm through distraction only maintains that calm until the entertainment loses its interest.

Delusions and hallucinations are a major cause of a distracted mind and are the result of undigested experiences, ideas and beliefs that have no bearing on reality. Often these are created through past trauma or the acceptance of faulty information from a perceived "trusted" source. An enlightened person has come to terms with all their delusions and hallucinations and discarded them.

One method for dissolving delusions and hallucinations is through detached observation of the thoughts and feelings one experiences and then releasing what is no longer useful and serves no purpose in the present. After superconscious meditation practice one can reflect on life and ask, with expectation of receiving the answer, "Do all of my beliefs and ideas about life serve my process of Self-realization?" Those beliefs and ideas that do not serve the enlightenment process can be seen for what they are, no longer useful, and released.

To have a tangled mind means that thoughts are not separated from emotions or feelings. Thoughts then run through the mind, and various emotional states are triggered. One may be sitting outside in a beautiful outdoor setting and a thought of a past experience that is attached to an unpleasant emotional state may pass through the mind. One immediately re-experiences that emotional state, despite the fact it has no bearing on the present. Yet the present experience may become colored by that emotional state. Until control of the mind returns, all actions will be taken from that state and most likely be inappropriate.

Similarly, a mind directed by cravings will not process reality clearly. Cravings churn up the mind into focusing on either acquiring what is desired or avoiding what is not desired. This kind of focus shuts out the ability to function within the whole of reality. When cravings are in effect, reality becomes fragmented into an all-encompassing mission to satisfy the craving. Then one is cut off from the source of wisdom-impelled action.

A clear and controlled mind can reflect the reality of what is presented to it. This is wisdom. The mind is neither "attached to" nor "identified with" what is presented to it. In this way, the mind can do its job of observing the world, clearly communicating with the soul, and receiving and translating soul impulses into action within the world. Nothing then is rejected or longed for, maintaining clarity of awareness. What is, is, and can be related to appropriately.

II.14 "Inquiry (the second gate keeper to liberation) should be undertaken by an intelligence that has been purified by a close study of the scripture, and this inquiry should be unbroken. By such inquiry the intelligence becomes keen and is able to realize the supreme; hence inquiry alone is the best remedy for long lasting illness known as samsara. What is inquiry? To inquire thus "Who am I? How has this samsara come into being?" is true inquiry. Knowledge of truth arises from such inquiry; from such knowledge there follows tranquility in oneself; and then there arises the supreme peace that passeth understanding and the ending of all sorrow. (Inquiry is not reasoning or analyses; it is directly looking into oneself.)

When one does not fully comprehend what one is in truth, or what the world appearance is in reality, there is difficulty functioning appropriately within time and space. It can be done, but it is clumsy and difficult, with the potential of experiencing many sorrows that are unnecessary. This is the experience of the average human consciousness not interested in actualizing the fullest potential for development.

Inquiry into the truth of what one is, in essence, is the supreme means to realizing enlightenment. The practice of inquiry is most effective for one of a purified intelligence. By knowing one's true nature and living in that knowledge, one goes beyond sorrow to embody the peace of fully liberated consciousness.

The first step in the practice of inquiry requires the release of false information one has about one's Self and the process of spiritual enlightenment. This occurs by the study of information presented by enlightened people. The study of such information provides explanations and insights about the nature of consciousness. Through meditating on the information, with the intention of attuning one's consciousness with the source of the information, one can then grasp the meaning through direct transmission of the knowledge studied.

With continued practice one can evaluate progress made by the lessening of dissonance within life experiences. As one lives from the knowledge provided by enlightened teachers, and gains direct experience with the results of living in an enlightened way, life becomes lighter and more enjoyable because of being less burdened by delusions and hallucinations. The intelligence becomes sharper, clearer and more easily discerns truth from falsehood. Once one's intelligence becomes sufficiently free of attachment to beliefs and ideas that do not serve the enlightenment process, direct inquiry into the nature of consciousness can begin.

After meditation practice, when the mind is calm and clear, is the best time for intensive Self-inquiry. Remaining in the silence after meditation, one directs attention to the central part of the body, from the sacrum to the top of the skull, and gently asks, "What am I at the core of my being? What is my real relationship with the life experiences I have? What am I beyond the names and forms I experience in this life?" Feeling these or similar questions gently resonating within, one then simply waits in the silence for the answer, maintaining trust that the answers will be provided. This will occur either during the session of intensive inquiry or as a flash of insight later on.

When participating in daily activities the practice of inquiry is maintained by remaining aware of thoughts, feelings, emotions and experiences, through relaxed observation, and always wondering, "What is it that experiences this?" This assists one in learning to refrain from identifying with the body, mind and transient phenomena. Living in this way retrains awareness to focus on what it is, an eternal witnessing consciousness, and not what it is not, the ever-changing fluctuations of name and form.

II.15 "Contentment is another gate keeper to liberation. He who has quaffed the nectar of contentment does not relish cravings for sense pleasures; no delight in the world is as sweet as contentment, which destroys all sins. What is contentment? To remove all cravings for what is not obtained unsought and to be satisfied with what comes unsought, without being elated or depressed even by them, this is contentment. As long as one is not satisfied in the self, he will be subjected to sorrow."

To be contented without dependency on pleasures found in time and space is the highest form of happiness. The idea that contentment arises from people, places, things or experiences is a false notion. Contentment sought from this understanding is considered "sinful" because it will always eventually lead to pain in one way or another. Satisfaction derived from remaining stable in the Self promotes clarity of awareness for one that is not yet fully spiritually awake and maintains enlightened understanding for one already awake to the Self.

Much spiritual strength results from the development of content in all circumstances. Fearlessness, an essential quality for any spiritual aspirant, is the natural result of remaining content in the Self. When one neither craves to gain. nor disapproves of loss in the passing things of life, fear has no grounds to take hold. The neutrality that contentment engenders allows one to see things clearly and take action within this clarity when necessary.

Fearlessness and neutrality frees one's being from acting out of compulsion. If one's life is directed by compulsion, there is no freedom, because there is no choice. A liberated soul is directed only by the intelligence of the Self, not by subconscious guilt, fear or cravings. A mind that is free of compulsion does not whirl endlessly in a hurricane of thoughts determined to analyze, achieve or prevent anything, thereby drowning out the natural intelligence of being. Centered in the silence of pure consciousness, all action and inaction will be appropriate because it is directed by intelligence beyond the mind that is wholly integrated with the entirety of the universe and not blinded by compulsion.

The Self is eternal and ever present. It is nowhere to be found because it is omniscient and omnipresent. The Self is everything that can be observed. It is the body, the thoughts in the mind, the emotions felt, the experiences of life, the people, the places and all things. The Self is the ground of being from which everything that can be observed manifests, and also the silence of enlightenment. The Self is the means by which all exist and are witnessed. If all is the Self, why be dissatisfied with anything?

Aligning one's understanding with this degree of contentment, the false sense of self as a tiny, limited, unhappy "me" naturally dissolves into the boundless field of pure consciousness. One then maintains a distinct viewpoint in time and space while embodied, while stable in the unlimited intelligence and wisdom of being an individualized, yet wholly integrated, unit of pure consciousness.

II.15 "Satsanga (company of the wise holy and enlightened persons) is yet another gate keeper to liberation. Satsanga enlarges one's intelligence, destroys one's ignorance and one's psychological distress. Satsanga is indeed superior to all other forms of religious practice like charity, austerity, pilgrimage, and the performance of religious rites."

People are influenced by each other's states of consciousness. An undisciplined person, in whom Self-mastery is not yet developed, can easily be disturbed by another's experiences of anger, grief, fear, guilt or similar negative feelings. Similarly, that same person can be uplifted by one whose awareness is clear and being is calm. By having the company of enlightened, or at the least functional, successful, drama-free people in life, one can benefit by being in the presence of their state of consciousness and having healthy minded role models to emulate. With continued contact with these types of people, one eventually begins to resonate at the same level, and experiences higher states of consciousness.

Enlightened people interact differently with the world than one who is confined to ego-sense. The actions of an enlightened person are not driven by fear or compulsion. By the study of authentic scriptures, the practice of transformational meditation and inquiry, accepting contentment in all circumstances, and attuning to the clear consciousness of teachers within an enlightenment tradition, the enlightened one has come to rest in his or her true nature and now lives from that viewpoint. Because of this, the enlightened person sees clearly what is experienced and reacts appropriately to life situations.

Surrounding, or at least attuning one's Self with those who function in life from such a viewpoint, clarifies one's own awareness and is superior to all other forms of spiritual practice. This is so because when one is in the presence of a fully awake person, or attuning to them in thought, one is in direct contact with pure consciousness. Paramahansa Yogananda once said to Roy Eugene Davis during his early discipleship, "Read a little, meditate more, and think of God all the time." With these words Yogananda was conveying the importance to attune to the state of pure consciousness (God) at all times.

Often, teachers will speak of the importance of maintaining attunement with the lineage of spiritual teachers one is connected to. They are not saying to worship or attune to the ego-sense, mind-body-personality of the teachers within the lineage. The teachers are indicating that one should attune to the state of consciousness the lineage represents. Again, this is a state of pure consciousness, the essence of one's being. The more frequent the experience of pure consciousness, the clearer one's own consciousness becomes, and one then awakes more rapidly to full spiritual liberation.

II.16 "These four –contentment, satsanga, the spirit of inquiry, and self control are the four surest means by which they who are drowning in the ocean of samsara can be saved. Contentment is the supreme gain. Satsanga is the best companion to the destination. The spirit of inquiry itself is the greatest wisdom. And self control is supreme happiness. If you are unable to resort to all these four, then practice one: by diligent practice of one of these, the others will also be found in you."

Spirituality is often burdened by ritualistic behavior and belief systems. All one ultimately needs to attain liberation of consciousness is a shift of viewpoint to accept that one is an unlimited unit of pure consciousness and then live from that perspective. The practice of contentment, surrounding oneself with supportive individuals, inquiring into one's true nature, and self-control support the enlightenment process until one is stable in Self-realization without question.

Implemented together, these four means to liberation provide rapid spiritual transformation. For those unable or unwilling to make the resolve to practice all four, the practice of only one will also develop the remaining three as they are all synergistically related. Contentment attracts the company of supportive people, self-control results in contentment, inquiry leads to self-control, spiritually resolved company engenders inquiry, and so on. Refraining from these practices will surely delay one's progress.

To delay the process of enlightenment is a waste of time and resources. While embodied and participating in the world, being as fully functional as possible supports the highest good. Not actualizing one's ability to function in the world in an enlightened, prosperous, helpful and healthy way because of compulsive fear of any kind is childish and not a quality of one intent on spirituality.

Relationships that are not supportive need to be discarded to make room for favorable relationships. Remaining in a relationship out of guilt, neediness, or any other debilitating dependent state, is not useful. Enlightened people are strong and enjoy the company of others of similar character. Supportive relationships foster strength not dependency.

Ideas and beliefs about what it means to be enlightened need to be inquired into to determine validity. Most information in the world about enlightenment is misleading. To determine truth from falsehood, one can inquire into the usefulness of information learned. That which appears useful can be tested for verification. Accepting on faith is only recommended once the source of information has been proven valid through inquiry and application. As one grows and realization becomes clearer, what may have been valid in the past may no longer remain valid for the present. Remaining open to the evolution of one's understanding is also essential.

Just as practice of any art or sport allows one to perform flawlessly and effortlessly, self-control allows one to accomplish goals with ease. By mastering the direction of one's life, one gains power to accomplish worthwhile goals. This then has a global effect on all aspects of one's action in the world. Participation in the world as an expression of the unlimited potential of the infinite consciousness draws one closer to realizing the essence of being.

Contentment promotes appropriate action in the world. When choices need made or actions taken, remaining content in the present allows one to act from a neutral place not colored by desire or aversion. Actions taken based on decisions made in a state of neutrality allow one to make the most appropriate choices that do not create more karma.

II.19 "Non recognition of the existence of Supreme peace in the heart and assumption of the reality of imaginary factors, are both born of imperfect knowledge and the consequence of perverted logic."

In this verse, what is referred to as the heart is the essence of one's being. It is the eternal spirit that is the foundation for all that is experienced in the world and the enlivening power of all life. Recognition of the Supreme peace within the heart requires one to keep awareness centered in the clear stillness of the spirit while functioning in the world. To not do so, fragments consciousness and leads one to mistake transient experiences for reality.

Reality (something that exists independently of all other things and from which all other things derive) *is* the essence of one's being. Much like when one dreams, everything within the dream *is* the dreamer and also the product of the imagination of the dreamer. The objects of perception in the world are products of the imagination of one's true Self.

To entertain the notion that the products of one's imagination is real, results in ignorance of one's true Self and is the cause of misunderstanding about the nature of reality. The more attention given to the transient things of the world, the less attention is given to the eternal changeless nature of one's own spirit, resulting in less peace and more attachment to things that cannot last. Further, this blurs the clarity needed to remain fully awake to what is real.

Knowing that the world of experience is ultimately imaginary does not require a denial of the world. The objects of perception are to be related to appropriately as they are experienced. The purpose of acquiring flawless knowledge about what is, and what is not real, is to enable one to participate in the game of life without losing the perspective that it is a play of consciousness in the field of nature.

Remaining stable in the understanding of one's true nature requires training. Realizing one's enlightenment has a rich history of training opportunities. The study of authentic enlightenment scripture by writers of clear awareness provides ample reading material to study. From thousands of years past to the present, enlightened sages have taught those ready and willing to receive soul-liberating knowledge. Techniques to control the mind and return attention to one's spiritual essence have been devised for all temperaments. You only need to find the one for you.

The way is always open for those committed to walking it. To express one's enlightenment requires learning from credible sources and applying what is learned. Then through direct experience, the truth is revealed.

II.19 "Even as the ocean is the substratum of all waves, direct experience alone is the basis for all proofs- the direct experience of truth as it is."

Proofs (scriptures or teachings) that embody and point to enlightenment are born of direct experience of pure unconditioned truth. Pure consciousness embodies everything, and is the "truth as it is." Centered in one's essence as pure consciousness, one responds and acts appropriately in all situations. One's life then becomes an embodiment of the truth. Life, the proof, is then a constant direct experience and expression of the substratum and support of the source of all manifest and unmanifest things.

The common misconception is that the truth is an answer to a question. In reality, truth is a state of being. Thinking, debating, reasoning, or any other traditional method of finding the truth, can never satisfy the innate urge of the soul to restore its awareness to wholeness, because these processes never rise above the level of the mind. Truth encompasses the mind, but it is also beyond the mind.

Average awareness is filled with the constant rise and fall of emotions and an endless stream of thoughts. As long as these prevail, one usually cannot see beyond them. Thoughts and emotions contract awareness into a focus no bigger than the object of what the thoughts and emotions are about, the ego-sense. With thoughts and emotions silenced through spiritual practice, one can directly experience the truth of being pure infinite consciousness. When enlightened people share what they know, their teachings come from a state of directly experiencing the truth. One of the reasons having the company of enlightened people is so effective in assisting one's own spiritual growth is because they provide an immediate point of contact with that which one may not be able to access so easily. With repeated contact it becomes easier for one to experience pure consciousness directly. Then one knows what the enlightened teacher embodies and no words are necessary to convey or prove it. Explaining this to someone will never make complete sense until the person has direct experience.

To support this process requires trust in a spiritual teacher who embodies what he or she teaches. The restless mind can find an infinite number of ways to engender doubt about the validity of the process of enlightenment, thus sabotaging the chance of real spiritual growth. Having a teacher who speaks truthfully without pretense allows one to ignore the incessant stream of doubting thoughts to make way for the possibility of direct experience of reality as it is.

The enlightenment process is ultimately a personal matter. Authentic guidance is very helpful to facilitate one's own direct experience. Sharing thoughts and opinions about the subject with others who are not yet enlightened does not promote direct experience. Instead it keeps one functioning at the level of the ego-sense. To quicken enlightened awakening, it is best for one to do what is necessary to gain direct experience of one's own pure conscious nature and avoid that which confines awareness to only the mind and ego-sense.

III.11 "Rama said: Lord, during the cosmic dissolution, this world which is clearly seen now – where does it go?

Vasistha said: From where does the son of a barren woman come, and where does he go? A barren woman's son has no existence, ever. This analogy baffles you because you have taken the existence of the world for granted.

Consider this: Is there a bracelet - ness in the gold bracelet? Is there a thing called sky independent of the emptiness? Even so, there is no "thing" called the world independent of Brahman, the absolute. Just as coldness is inseparable from ice, what is called the world is inseparable from Brahman.

From the yogic perspective, the world appearance is formed from an interplay of three cosmic forces, Sattva: representing lightness, clarity, and an enlightened consciousness, Rajas: representing energy, change, and turbulence, and Tamas: representing inertia, darkness, and heaviness. When these three forces become imbalanced, the world appearance comes forth. At the end of a cycle of world manifestation, the world is said to dissolve back into a state of equilibrium in which nothing exists.

In this verse, Vasistha explains to Rama that ultimately the world goes nowhere during the cosmic dissolution. This is because the world is formed from eternal pure consciousness, here referred to as Brahman, the absolute. There is nothing that exists that is not Brahman, the absolute. Brahman, being the eternal absolute foundation of everything, is ever-present. States may change, but the pure consciousness always remains either modified or unmodified.

The analogy Vasistha uses of the gold bracelet is often used throughout the complete text of *Vasistha's Yoga*. It is intended to bring the point home that "everything is consciousness and that is all there is." The gold in a bracelet remains gold even if the bracelet were melted into a different form. The forms in consciousness remain consciousness, no matter how they may be experienced. The attributes given to the gold by calling it a bracelet does not change its essential nature as gold. Similarly, naming the forms in the world appearance is only a mental exercise and does not change the essential nature of consciousness.

Once one realizes that there is nothing more to know beyond that everything is consciousness, all that is left to do is live a natural life spontaneously and contentedly. In most cases it may take some time to come to terms with the fact that everything is consciousness. That is the purpose of spiritual practice, to slough off all mental debris and to expand awareness so that one can fully appreciate what it means that "everything is consciousness, and that is all there is."

Stable in this realization, because of having had understanding through direct experience, one can ask, "How am I living my eternal life and is it supportive of the evolution of consciousness?" If it is, then one can continue living centered in enlightenment. If it is not, one can find out what steps need to be taken for change, and then direct the life experience appropriately.

III.13 "Cosmic consciousness alone exists now and ever; in it are no worlds, no created beings. That consciousness reflected in itself appears to be creation. Even as an unreal nightmare produces real results, this world seems to give rise to a sense of reality in a state of ignorance. When true wisdom arises, this unreality vanishes."

Cosmic consciousness can be a state of expansive awe, lost in timelessness or identified with the far reaches of the universe and creation. It can also be awareness of what is immediately present. Often when the concept of cosmic consciousness is brought to mind, we forget that the cosmos is every cell, molecule, breath and movement of the body. Even if we are only aware of the sun shining, the space between people in an office, or the feeling of the floor underneath of us while in meditation, that is still awareness of the cosmos and of consciousness.

The human body has a nervous system that gathers and collects information from the senses, and brings it to the mind. The mind then makes sense of what we experience. Yoga practice endeavors to refine that nervous system, in such a way that it may process consciousness with the utmost clarity. Meditation trains the mind to be still, that pure awareness may be realized fully, beyond the distraction of ordinary human consciousness.

It needs to be said that there is nothing wrong with ordinary human consciousness. It is as much the Self as anything else. And that may very well be the first (and only) step in awakening, to make peace with our ordinary human consciousness. Yet, our consciousness is as vast or as small as we make it. We have the capacity to live identified with the wholeness of life, as an expansive, rich and beautiful being — what most people refer to as Cosmic Consciousness. We can experience every world and everyone as our very Self. In this way, realize there are no other worlds or beings other than our Self! Then we experience consciousness as experiencer and consciousness as experience. They are the same, one whole thing.

Consciousness as Experience + Consciousness as Experiencer = Consciousness

Realization of Consciousness as Experience + Realization of Consciousness as Experiencer = A Liberated Being

Making peace with the present moment and the fact the cosmos is us, right down to the smallest particle or pettiest thought, is the first step to realizing the rest of us — our expanded infinite expression. Then through the ripening process of time, or the ripening process of intentional yogic practices (or Kriyas), we become firmly established in the realization of Cosmic Consciousness (both big and small). We have the freedom to identify with whatever we like, be it a limited ego-centered personality, or the vastness of space and time as all things at once. The difference between a liberated being and one that is "bound" is their freedom to identify and BE with whatever aspect of themselves they choose.

It has been and always will be true, that there is only one reality. Sometimes, when identified with a small-limited personality, this truth is forgotten. Then thoughts of death disturb us, fear of loss causes us pain, craving for something we don't think we have makes us anxious. As we calm our minds and learn to relax in the present, we open up space for the light of what has always been true to shine in. This light is knowledge. When we know for certain that all life is us, that every thing is an image of our own consciousness, and that there is nothing we can lose that will take away from what we are, all mental disturbance and agitation dissolves. We are left with what is left, the only thing there is — our eternal and infinite Self, identified with what it likes, and this is the dawn of wisdom.

III.13 "By the apprehension of the perceived or the knowable, consciousness becomes the living soul and is apparently involved in repetitive history. When the false notion of a knowable apart from the knower (consciousness) ceases, it regains its equilibrium."

The soul, or the jiva, is the result of identifying with the world-appearance. Soul freedom results by letting go of the false idea that you are or have a soul, not by becoming aware of your soul. Being or having a soul is just another story we can tell ourselves, to keep the game of "repetitive history" or karma going.

The world-appearance is anything that is perceivable. Perception is defined as, "the act or faculty of apprehending by means of the senses or of the mind; cognition." The taste of your food, the smell of incense, the feeling of your clothes on your body, the sound of the wind through pine trees, and the sight of the book in your hand is perceivable. Also, the thoughts in your mind, the memories of your dreams, the feeling of safety, the emotions of anger and love, all these are perceivable too, and so are equally a facet of the world appearance. To realize that what is seen is the same as the seer promotes equilibrium and clarity in consciousness.

At first this can be a mental exercise. We can tell ourselves (our personality or the soul), that everything we see and experience is a direct reflection of our Self. The person across the street is us. The anger that our father shared, is us. The love we feel being around friends or our spouse, is us. The sky above and the ground below, is us. The stars thousands of light years away, are also our very being. We mentally affirm this. It is a beginning practice.

Then, by intentional meditation, we can encourage direct experience of this truth. Meditation, or other effective spiritual practices, help to calm the mind and balance the nervous system. This way we can sit still and tune into the infinite, which I like to call "the rest of us". It makes it easier to release attachment to the confined sense of Self that the personality is used to experiencing. Flowing our attention into a boundless thought free state, we contemplate that which we want to know.

Contemplation does not require thought. It only requires curiosity. Calm and centered, we can keep our attention in the higher brain centers, at the crown or the frontal lobe region and wonder, "What am I that is aware of all of these experiences, both external and internal?" Then we sit and wait. Wondering and contemplating in a state of interested curiosity stimulates "the rest of us" or the infinite portion of our Self, to respond. It is like running to get your heart rate up. You begin to run, and your body will respond by quickening your pulse. When you are curious and interested in something, and begin to contemplate that which you want to know, the body of your consciousness, or the infinite, responds by arranging the direct experience or realization of that contemplation.

When this direct experience finally dawns, false notions are seen for what they are, just like on waking up from a dream you know beyond a shadow of a doubt that it was only a dream. By direct experience of what you are, beyond thought and identification with only the perceivable, consciousness knows its peace, and the ever-present equilibrium is realized.

Then as you sit on your friend's porch, you hear the birds singing summer songs. You see the light reflecting off the lake. You feel the breeze cooling your skin, and it is all your very Self, not something happening outside of you. There is no need for thought. For the seer and the seen are one, and all is happening of its own accord.

Now you have a sense of the depth of contemplation possible through the examples above. Begin incorporating contemplation of your chosen sacred text into your daily spiritual practice sessions. Also consider continuing a general exploration of *Vasistha's Yoga* through contemplation of the excerpts below. No journaled reflection has been provided so that you may record your own thoughts.

The following passages have been chosen specifically because of their direct insight into the essence of the massive text that is *Vasistha's Yoga*. Once you feel comfortable grasping the meaning of these few passages, then consider studying Swami Venkatesananda's entire translation from cover to cover.

III.15 "*O Rama, even as from the waking state experience, there is no materiality in the objects seen in a dream (though while dreaming the objects appear to be solid) this world appears to be material yet in reality it is pure consciousness.*"

III.19 "*Death is but waking from a dream. Birth which arises from a wish is no more real than the wish, like waves in a mirage.*"

III.22 "*By the persistent practice egotism is quieted. Then you will naturally rest in your consciousness; and the perceived universe heads towards the vanishing point. What is called practice?*

Thinking of that alone, speaking of that, conversing of that with one another, utter dedication to that one alone – this is called practice by the wise. When one's intellect is filled with beauty and bliss, when one's vision is broad, when passion for sensual enjoyment is absent in one – that is practice. When one is firmly established in the conviction that this universe has never even been created, and therefore does not exist as such, and when thoughts like "This is world, this I am" do not arise at all in one – that is practice."

III.27 "*Until the consciousness of duality is completely dispelled, you cannot act in the infinite consciousness; you cannot even understand it, even as one standing in the sun does not know the coolness of the shade of a tree.*"

III.40 "In reality, what is mental activity but consciousness, and that consciousness is the supreme truth."

III.42 "This universe is but a long dream. The ego sense and also the fancy that there are others, are as real as dream objects. The sole reality is the infinite consciousness, which is omnipresent, pure, tranquil, omnipotent and whose very body and being is absolute consciousness (therefore not an object, not knowable): wherever this consciousness manifests in whatever manner, it is that. Because the substratum (the infinite consciousness) is real, all that is based on it acquire reality, though the reality is of the substratum alone."

III.44 "What is reflected in one's consciousness shines outside also."

III.56 "This is a well known truth: whatever be one's consciousness, that one is. Things (objects or substances) come into being on account of one's fancy (thought or idea); and one's fancy also arises from things. Poison turns into nectar through one's fancy (or faith); even so, an unreal object or substance becomes real when such intense faith is present. Without a cause no effect is produced anywhere at any time; and therefore there is no fancy or thought either.

III.57 "This fanciful conviction that the unreal is real is deep rooted by repeated imagination."

III.60 "A man is pulled in two different directions: towards the realization of Brahman the absolute and towards the ignorant acceptance of the reality of the world. That which he strives to realize with great intensity wins! Once he overcomes ignorance, the deluded vision of the unreal is forever dispelled."

III.61 "Just as there is no division between a bracelet and gold, no division between waves and water, there is no division between the universe and infinite consciousness. The latter alone is the universe; the universe as such is not the infinite consciousness, just as bracelet is made of gold but gold is not made of bracelet."

III.88 "One beholds with physical eyes only such objects as have been created by him in his own mind, naught else...A person is made of whatever is firmly established as the truth of his being in his own mind: that he is, naught else."

III.89 "If the mind is fully saturated with something, what ever happens to the body does not effect the mind. The mind is unaffected even by boons and curses, even as the firmly established mountain is not moved by horns of the little beast. The body does not create mind, but the mind creates the body."

III.91 "Whatever appears in one's consciousness, that seems to come into being, gets established and even bears fruit. Such is the power of the mind."

III.95 "There is no division between mind and action. Before it is projected as action it arises in the mind, with the mind itself as its 'body'. Hence, action is nothing but the movement of energy in consciousness, and it inevitably bears its own fruit. When such action comes to an end, mind comes to an end too; and when the mind ceases, there is no action. This applies only to the liberated sage, not others."

III.98 "The pure mind is free of latent tendencies, and therefore it attains Self-knowledge. Since this entire universe is within the mind, the notions of bondage and liberation are also within it."

III.101 "This world is nothing but pure hallucination. It is nothing more than an idea. In the infinite consciousness the ideas of creation arose: and that is what is. O Rama, this world is nothing more than an idea; all the objects of consciousness in this world are just ideas; reject the error of ideation and be free of ideas; and remain rooted in truth, attain peace."

III.110 "The mind experiences what it itself constructs, the mind is nothing but what has been put together by thought, knowing this, do as you please."

III.110 "Just as an actor is able to portray himself as the character of different personalities, the mind is able to create different states of consciousness like waking and dreaming."

III.111 "There is no other path to one's salvation, except control over one's mind, which means resolute effort to abandon cravings in the mind."

III.112 "First destroy the mental conditioning by renouncing cravings; and then remove from your mind even *the concepts of bondage and liberation. Be totally free of conditioning."*

III.114 "Ideas and thoughts are bondage; and their coming to an end is liberation. Therefore be free of them and do what has to be done spontaneously...What the mind seeks to attain, that the senses strive for with all their energy."

III.118 "The highest state of consciousness can be attained by all, even by animals and by primitive men, by those who have a body and even by disembodied beings, for it involves only the rise of wisdom."

III.121 "When the division between the seer, the sight and the seen is abolished, that is the supreme. When the mind travels from one country to another, between them is cosmic intelligence. Be that always. Your true nature is distinct from the limited wakeful state, dreaming and sleep consciousness; it is eternal, unknowable, not inert, remain that always."

III.122 "The seemingly endless stream of ignorance can be crossed over only by constant company of holy ones. From such company there arises wisdom concerning what is worth seeking and what is to be avoided. Then there arises the pure wish to attain liberation. This leads to serious inquiry. Then the mind becomes subtle because the inquiry thins out the mental conditioning. As a result of the rising of pure wisdom, one's consciousness moves in the reality. Then the mental conditioning vanishes and there is non attachment. Bondage to actions and their fruits ceases. The vision is firmly established in truth and the apprehen-

sion of the unreal is weakened. Even while living and functioning in this world, he who has this unconditional vision does what has to be done as if asleep, without thinking of the world and its pleasure. After some years of living like this, one is fully liberated and transcends all these states: he is liberated while living."

III.122 "It is only for the sake of scriptural instruction that one speaks of the Self, Brahman, etc., but in truth one alone is."

IV.2, 2 "Hence, it is pure foolishness to assume that there exists a causal relationship between Brahman and the world: the truth is that Brahman alone exists and what appears to be the world is that alone."

IV.2, 3 "There is no cause and effect relation between the supreme being and the universe."

IV.11 "For, the self is what it considers itself to be. In fact, there is neither bondage nor liberation for the lord. I do not know how these notions of bondage and liberation have come into being! There is neither bondage nor liberation, only that infinite being is seen: yet the eternal is veiled by the transient, and this is indeed a great wonder (or a great illusion)."

IV.12, 13 "O sage, gods, demons and human beings are non different from this cosmic ocean of consciousness known as Brahman: this is the truth, all other assertions are false. They (the gods, etc.) entertain false notions (like "I am not the absolute") and thus superimpose on themselves impurity and the feeling of downfall. Even they dwell forever in this cosmic ocean of consciousness; yet considering themselves separated from Brahman, they are deluded. Though they are ever pure, they superimpose impurity on themselves and this is the seed of all their actions and their consequences, viz., happiness, unhappiness, ignorance, and enlightenment."

"All beings here in this world obtain only those actions which spring from the storehouse of their own potentialities and predispositions: no one else is responsible for their actions, no superhuman being or god."

IV.15 "As long as there is the body, so long shall pain be painful and pleasure pleasant: but the wise are not attached to either. Rejoicing in joy and suffering in suffering, the great ones appear to behave like the ignorant, though in fact they are enlightened."

"O Rama, renounce all cravings and longings and do what needs to be done in the realization that you are ever the pure infinite consciousness."

IV.17 "That mind is pure in which all cravings are in a state of quiescence. What ever the pure mind wishes, that materializes."

"Rama asked: 'How did the succession of births, etc., arise in the mind of Sukra?'

"Vasistha replied: 'Sukra had been taught by his father Bhrgu concerning the succession of births, and this teaching had conditioned Sukra's mind which conjured up the expansion of such conditioning. Only when the mind is totally purified of all conditioning does it regain its utter purity; that pure mind experiences liberation."

IV.18 "One should enquire into that which is truly the uncaused cause of all substances, which is yet beyond all such causation: this alone is worth enquiring into, for this alone is the essential. Why enquire into the non-essential?"

"It is only when the division between the seer and the seen is given up, only when the two are 'seen' as of only one substance, that the truth is realized."

"A painted pot of nectar is not nectar, nor a painted flame fire, and a painting of a woman is not a woman: wise words are mere words (ignorance) not wisdom, unless they are substantiated by absence of desire and anger."

IV.19 "Upon their appearance as the jiva, whatever type of contemplation they adopt, they soon become of the same nature...Hence, one should resort to that which is not limited, conditioned or finite."

IV. 32 "Adhering to the injunctions of the scripture one should patiently wait for perfection which comes in its own time...Inquire constantly into the nature of truth, knowing that 'this is but a reflection'. Do not be led by others; only animals are led by others. Wake up from the slumber of ignorance. Wake up and strive to end old age and death."

IV.33 "However, the higher form of 'I-ness' which gives rise to the feeling 'I am one with the entire universe; there is nothing apart from me', is the understanding of the enlightened person. Another type of 'I-ness' is when one feels that the 'I' is extremely subtle and atomic in nature and therefore different from and independent of everything in the universe: this, too, is unobjectionable, being condu-

cive to liberation...By the persistent cultivation of the higher form of 'I-ness' the lower form is eradicated.

"Having kept the lower 'I-ness' in check, one should resort to the higher form of 'I-ness', persistently generating in oneself the feeling: 'I am the All' or 'I am extremely subtle and independent'. In due course even this higher form of 'I-ness' should be completely abandoned. Then one may either engage oneself in all activity or remain in seclusion: there is no fear of downfall for him."

IV. 46 "The nature of the wise person is not to desire those experiences which one does not effortlessly obtain, and to experience those which have already arrived. If one is able to wean the mind away from craving for sense-pleasure by whatever means, one is saved from being drowned in the ocean of delusion. He who has realized his oneness with the entire universe, and who has thus risen above both desire 'for' and desire 'against', is never deluded."

"He who is not attracted by the pleasure of either this world or of heaven (whether or not there is body consciousness in him) is liberated, even if he does not specifically desire or strive for such liberation."

IV. 53 "Even if one engages oneself in every other sort of spiritual endeavor, and even if one has the gods themselves as one's teachers, and even if one were in heaven or any other region, liberation is not had except through the cessation of all notions."

IV. 62 "Rama, you are already a liberated being: live like one!"

V. 5 "All this is but the reflection of the truth. Nothing but the one Brahman exists. 'I am different from this' is pure fancy: give it up, O Rama. The one self perceives itself within itself as the infinite consciousness. Therefore, there is no sorrow, no delusion, no birth (creation), nor creature: whatever is, is. Be free from distress, O Rama. Be free of duality; remain firmly established in the self, abandoning even concern for your own welfare. Be at peace within, with a steady mind. Let there be no sorrow in your mind. Rest in the inner silence. Remain alone, without self willed thoughts. Be brave, having conquered the mind and the senses. Be desireless, content with what comes to you unsought. Live effortlessly, without grabbing or giving up anything. Be free from all mental perversions and from the blinding taint of illusion. Rest content in your own self. Thus, be free from all distress. Remain in an expansive state in the self, like the full ocean. Rejoice in the self by the self, like the blissful rays of the full moon."

V.13 "Consciousness minus conceptualization is the eternal Brahman, the absolute; consciousness plus conceptualization is thought. A small part of it, as it were, is seated in the heart as reality. This is known as the finite intelligence or individualized consciousness. However, this limited consciousness soon 'forgot' its own essential conscious nature and continued to be, but inert. It then became the thinking faculty with reception and rejection as its inherent tendencies. In fact, it is the infinite consciousness alone that has become all this: but until it awakens to its infinite nature, it does not know itself in self-knowledge. Hence, the mind should be awakened by means of inquiry based on scripture, dispassion, and control of the senses. This intelligence when it is awakened shines as Brahman the absolute; or else it continues to experience this finite world."

V.14 "O Rama, he who comes forward to remove the sorrow of people of perverted intelligence is endeavoring to cover the sky with a small umbrella. They who behave like beasts cannot be instructed, for they are being led like animals by the rope of their own mind. Indeed, even stones shed tears, looking at those ignorant people, who sink in the mire of their own mind, whose actions spell their own doom. Hence, the wise man does not attempt to teach those who have not overcome their own mind and are therefore miserable in every way. On the other hand, the wise do endeavor to remove the sorrow of those who have conquered their mind and who are therefore ripe to undertake self-inquiry."

"Realizing 'I am not' and 'this is not' remain firm and unmoved, like the infinite space. Abandon the impure thought which creates a duality of self – world. In the middle between the self as the seer and the world as the seen, you are the seeing (sight): always remain in this realization. Between the experiencer and the experience you are the experiencing: knowing this remain in self-knowledge."

V.15 "When the self, self-forgetfully identifies itself with the objects seen and experienced and is thus impurified, there arises the poison of craving...Whatever terrible suffering and calamities there are in the world are all the fruits of craving, O Rama. When this craving has ceased one's life force is pure and all divine qualities and virtues enter one's heart.

"Therefore, O Rama, give up craving by giving up thinking or conceptualization. The mind cannot exist with-

out thinking or conceptualization. First, let the images of 'I', 'you', and 'this' not arise in the mind, for it is because of these images that hopes and expectation come into being. If you can thus refrain from building these images, you will also be counted as a man of wisdom. Craving is non different from ego-sense. Ego sense is the source of all sins. Cut at the very root of this ego sense with the sword of wisdom of the non-ego. Be free from fear."

V.17 "Once the realization that 'I am the self of all' has arisen one does not again fall into error or sorrow. It is this self alone which is variously described as the void, nature, Maya, Brahman, consciousness, Siva, Purusha, etc. That alone is ever real; there is naught else. Resort to the understanding of non duality. The reality is neither duality (for it is the mind that creates division) nor unity (for the concept of unity arises from its antithesis of duality). When these concepts cease, the infinite consciousness alone is realized to be the sole reality."

V.18 "O Rama, all beings are your relatives, for in this universe there does not exist absolute unrelatedness. The wise know that 'There is nowhere I am not' and 'That is not which is not mine': thus they overcome limitation and conditioning."

V.21 "Craving is the root of all sorrow, O Rama: and the only intelligent way is to renounce all cravings completely and not to indulge them. Even as a fire burns all the more fiercely when fed with fuel, thoughts multiply by thinking: thoughts cease only by the extinction of thinking... The mind attains fulfillment only by utter dispassion, not by filling it with desires and hopes... The light of the full moon is not as bright nor is the ocean as full nor the face of the Goddess of prosperity as radiant as the mind free of craving…When the mind is free from movements of thought (which are motivated by hopes and cravings) then it becomes no-mind: and that is liberation…Hence, for restoring peace to the mind, remove the disturbing cause, which is hope or craving."

V.24 Bali asked: "Father, kindly tell me what intelligent practice will enable me to conquer the mind."

Virocana replied: "The very best intelligent means by which the mind can be subdued is complete freedom from desire, hope, or expectation in regard to all objects at all times. It is by this means that this powerful elephant (the mind) can be subdued. This means is both very easy and extremely difficult, my son: it is very difficult for one who is not earnest in his effort. There is no harvest without sowing: the mind is not subdued without persistent practice. Hence, take up this practice of renunciation. Until one turns away from sense pleasure here, one will continue to roam in the world of sorrow. Even a strong man will not reach his destination if he does not move toward it. No one can reach the state of total dispassion without persistent practice."

V.26 Bali asked Sukra: "Lord, it is the reflection of your own divine radiance that prompts me to place this problem before you. I have no desire for pleasure; and I wish to learn the truth. Who am I? Who are you? What is this world? Please tell me all this."

Sukra replied: "I am on my way to another realm, O Bali: but I shall give you in a few words the very quintessence of wisdom. Consciousness alone exists, conscious-

ness alone is all this, all this is filled with consciousness. I, you, and all this world, are but consciousness. If you are humble and sincere, you will gain everything from what I have said; if not, an attempt at further explanation will be like pouring oblations into a heap of ashes (i.e., useless; the oblations are meaningful only when poured into the sacred fire). The objectivity (conceptualization) of consciousness is known as bondage and the abandonment of such objectivity is liberation. Consciousness minus such objectivity is the reality of everything: this is the conviction of all philosophies. When you are established in this vision, you will also attain the infinite consciousness. I shall now depart to do the work of the gods; for as long as the body lasts, one shall not abandon appropriate action."

VI.2:42 "What is IS the infinite consciousness."

VI.2:42 "Nirvana, or liberation, is the non-experience of ego sense."

VI.2:42 "The ignorant sees the world as physical reality, the wise as consciousness. To the wise there is neither ego sense nor the world."

VI.2:42 "Conditioning alone is the mind, which ceases when inquired into.

VI.2:47 "In this world contentment alone is the best medicine, the best tonic and greatest good fortune. The content heart is ready for enlightenment. First turn away from worldliness, then resort to satsanga, inquire into the truth of scripture and cultivate disinterest in pleasure and you will attain the supreme truth."

VI.2:48 "The supreme state is that which is."

Chapter Ten

YOGIC SLEEP

Yogic sleep is a method of realizing the continuation of Self through all states of consciousness. It is popularly referred to as Yoga Nidra and is often understood as only a method of deep relaxation experienced after an intensive Hatha Yoga session. Yogic sleep is much more than a quiet interlude of physical relaxation. It gives one the ability to remain aware while sleeping and dreaming. Through this awareness one can learn to consciously experience the transition from life into death, and then back into life again. Suffice it to say, this capacity greatly reduces or even eliminates humanities deepest fear, that of annihilation after the body dies.

Learning to practice yogic sleep is a necessary step in making our entire life a consecrated example of full spiritual liberation. The hours we sleep are not intended to be a time of mindless oblivion. It is the body that needs sleep, not your eternal ever-present consciousness. As we learn to maintain our awareness throughout active daily living, as well as in the moments in which our bodies rest, it becomes easier to appreciate the totality of our being.

Our first experiences with yogic sleep may occur after a Hatha Yoga session. Most Hatha Yoga teachers are trained to end sessions in corpse pose, lying on one's back with palms up, with arms and legs 10 to 20 degrees out from the midline. This procedure helps to integrate and reset the nervous system. It can provide deep relaxation and rest that is sorely need for most people in our current era. However, this is not yogic sleep in its proper form. It is a method of relaxation and an excellent means of preparing for yogic sleep.

As mentioned previously, Yoga for the purpose of Self-realization is meant to be undertaken by people who are already relatively healthy and well-adjusted. When we are well-rested and know how to meditate sitting in an upright position, we can explore yogic sleep in its proper function. This is because you have to be able to meditate sitting upright, before you will be able to remain superconscious while lying down. Even when people sit upright and meditate, the majority of them will fall asleep at some point.

When not deprived of sleep and with a body that is already relaxed and healthy, the yogi may lay down and train herself to maintain awareness as the body falls asleep. Then the yogi's consciousness can remain, observing all the changes within the mind and dreams, fully aware of one's sense of Self as pure consciousness. This takes practice. It is a very subtle process to train one's Self to remain conscious, when our cultural and ancestral habit is to drift into unconscious sleep as the body relaxes. We will discuss the subtle process and methods at the end of this section. For now, let's consider some profound possibilities of Self-development related to yogic sleep.

Many have alluded to the idea that yoga can lead one into a state of immortality. This is true, but not in the sense most understand. The immortality of yoga arises by identifying fully with the eternal Self. It is not achieved by keeping the physical body of cells, organs and tissues alive indefinitely. So long as we are obsessed with or identified with a limited physical form, such as the body, we will not be able to appreciate the full glory of our divine consciousness. To aim to sustain a physical body eternally, would be the equivalent of trying to maintain one particular body you inhabited in a dream throughout infinity. The true yogi does not desire this, because the yogi is identified with the dreamer and not the rising and falling bodies within the dream.

Learning to experience superconsciousness as the body sleeps gives one a direct realization that the physical body is not necessary for the activity of life to be perceived. As the strength of this realization grows, one can also develop the capacity to explore the depths of consciousness beyond the habit of considering the physical world to be the only permanent reality.

My Kriya Yoga teacher was once asked, "It has been said that at the moment of death, if one can keep attention at the crown chakra, that person will be fully liberated and able to dissolve into the divine oneness. How can I be sure that I am liberated at the moment of death?" My teacher replied by intimating that the only way you can be certain of spiritual liberation at the moment of death, is by being liberated fully while alive. This is a profound statement in many ways. On one hand it shows that we are not to be focused on a period of death in the future, but to focus right now on our present state of liberation. It can also carry over to our understanding of waking life and the dream state as the body sleeps.

The contents of dreams are a reflection of our waking life. The qualities of dreams are the same as the qualities of our daily experience. This will be true in death, as well. The experiences we have after death will be a reflection of our experiences in life. The reflections in one state influence the reflections in the other. This is why working with our dream life can be so profound. By changing our waking life thoughts, actions, emotions and habits, we change our dream content. By doing dream work we learn to be aware during dreaming and to change the contents of the dream. In this way, we also impact the experiences in the waking state. This is the foundation of Tibetan Dream Yoga and the work of active imagination made popular by Carl Jung. It has relevance in many other cultures, as well. It is also applicable to our work as a Kriya Yogi.

The common belief is that dreams are only the result of our accumulated impressions of the day, or that what we do while alive determines our after-death states. That is true, but it also goes the other way. What we do in our dreams impacts our waking life. What we experience after death determines our next birth. If we are unconscious while dreaming, we are probably equally unconscious while waking. If we are at the mercy of our karmic impressions after the body dies, we were also at the mercy of our karmic impressions while living.

Here is a quote from Vasistha's Yoga we considered in the last chapter of this book:

II.3 "Countless have been the universes that have come into being and dissolved. In fact even the countless universes that exist at this moment are impossible to conceive of. All this can immediately be realized in one's own heart, for these universes are the creation of the desire that arises in the heart like castles built in the air. The living being conjures up this world in his heart and while he is alive he strengthens this illusion; when he passes away he conjures up the world beyond and experiences it- thus there arises worlds within worlds just as there are layers within layers of a plantain stem. Neither the worlds of matter, nor the modes of creation are truly real; yet the living and the dead think and feel they are real. Ignorance of this truth keeps up appearances."

Can you believe that? Maybe? No? Yes? The good news is, it's not a question of belief. This understanding becomes clear the more experienced you become as a meditator and yogi. This is because yoga removes the ignorance that keeps up appearances. It cannot be helped in the same way that dirt cannot stay on your feet if you apply soap, hot water and scrub your skin.

We practice Kriya meditation to train ourselves to realize our relationship to our body, personality, history and life experiences. This relationship is temporary. Once we can see this relationship, we then practice Vichara to get a full sense of who or what we actually are as pure consciousness. We practice yogic sleep to train ourselves to remain fully present as our body and mind moves through cycles of rest and activity. This training takes us to the point of being able to even be aware of the cycles of life (activity) and death (rest).

Once we have developed these capacities, we can work to fully embody the wisdom in the above quote from Vasistha. What is that wisdom? It is the wisdom to realize fully that:

"Countless have been the universes that have come into being and dissolved. In fact even the countless universes that exist at this moment are impossible to conceive of."

That the rise and fall of universal perception and experience is eternal, unending. That the mind cannot understand or conceive of the scope of such interaction between the form and formless. This is also true of our dreaming. The dreams rise and fall endlessly.

"All this can immediately be realized in one's own heart, for these universes are the creation of the desire that arises in the heart like castles built in the air. The living being conjures up this world in his heart and while he is alive he strengthens this illusion; when he passes away he conjures up the world beyond and experiences it- thus there arises worlds within worlds just as there are layers within layers of a plantain stem."

That once you know your heart, your essence, you will see that the world experience that seems so real to you is a direct reflection of your heart's desires. That the afterlife is also created by your desires and habitual imaginations, either chosen consciously or provided for you by your culture or ancestry. From the heart we witness our dreams, both during our waking hours and during sleep. Learning to identify as the heart, whether awake or asleep, we know the dream and our relationship to it. We are not bound by it or unconsciously drown in its activities.

"Neither the worlds of matter, nor the modes of creation are truly real; yet the living and the dead think and feel they are real. Ignorance of this truth keeps up appearances."

That what we think and feel is real is only so due to ignorance. It is this ignorance that keeps up our experience of the world appearance. When we are ignorant of the fact we are dreaming, our worst nightmares and wildest fantasies cannot be disputed as an actual reality.

This can be illustrated in the varied views and illusions different people, cultures and disciplines support. Some biblical scientists say the world is only 6,000 years old. Some physical scientists say it is 4.5 billion years. Some people say disease is caused by germs, by spirits, by erratic life force energy, by eating the wrong foods, by poisons, by genetics or by unresolved traumas or wrong thinking. In astrology, some people claim the tropical zodiac is correct. Others will say the sidereal zodiac is correct. Still others will say astrology is totally invalid. Each will find a reason to support their claims and ignore those who do not support their claim. In the end, every individual will live their life based on the beliefs held within their heart. This keeps up the reality of a temporary appearances. This builds the structure for the dream each one of us experiences.

As we mature, the realization that objectivity is an illusion becomes clear. This is facilitated by your Kriya Yoga Vichara practice and made clear by your practice of yogic sleep. As the realization arises, that the observer (the subject) and the observed (the object) are really one and the same, you begin to awaken to the fullness of your consciousness. Then you find no difference between your sleeping dreams and your waking life. They are experienced as different states of the same reality.

This may begin in your dreams as you sleep. You may find that as you sleep, you begin to know more often that you are dreaming. You may not be able to alter or change the dream, but you know for certain you are dreaming. Instead of being unconsciously caught up in and watching the story of the dream, you know you are it.

This is similar to becoming more conscious in your waking life. At first you may not be able to stop your moods or alter your life course, but there comes a time when it is as if you become an observer. You are watching your life happen from somewhere outside of the experience. Instead of flying into a rage when angered, you see yourself beginning to grow angry. It is no longer automatic. Or instead of getting lost in the bliss of a happy moment, until you finally realize it's over, you become the observer that timelessly savors all of the present moment joy. It is the accumulation of your yogic practices that begins to create this lucidity both in waking and in sleeping.

Now the question arises, how can I become lucid while sleeping? How can I remain as the eternal witnessing presence without slipping into unconsciousness as my body sleeps? What would it be like to remain as fully awake in my consciousness while my body takes its rest in sleep? It requires similar skills as you have been developing in your meditation — the skill of maintaining your attention and focus no matter what your body feels or your mind thinks. It requires you are able to hold your attention on one point of concentration, using your will, while letting go of all other distractions. In this situation, the distraction is that of a sleeping body and the tendency toward unconsciousness as the body rests.

My first experiences with superconscious, or lucid sleep, occurred when I was a teenager. I remember thinking it was strange and did not understand what was happening. It was quite disorienting. The world was vivid and real, and I was aware it was a dream world. I could observe, and I knew that what was happening in the dream was not really affecting the real "me," but I did not know how long the experience would last or where it was leading.

When I was 21, after a year of practicing intensive Kriya Meditation, I had another superconscious sleep experience. It occurred as I fell asleep listening to a lecture on maintaining awareness in the body as a tool for spiritual growth. I was not expecting it. I felt the same, as if I was awake, but then realized I was snoring and my body was asleep. I could still think, ponder and feel, while maintaining a sense of existence. I existed, but as an observer of everything, even my sleeping body. Then dreams started. For most of the night I remained in this state. Aware of my body, aware of my dreams and aware of myself as an observer. It was not as disorienting as the experiences I had as a teenager. That was because I was used to this state. I accessed it every morning in meditation.

It was then I realized the value of sleeping superconsciously. When you are aware while the body sleeps, you can choose to continue your meditation practices throughout the night! You can consciously explore your relationship with divinity, without the need to cater to a body. Now, you can quicken your spiritual awakening process by having the late hours of the night to continue your inner work. Why is this? Because just like in meditation, you are learning to direct your consciousness to that which you want to know, and you can do the same in sleep.

When you sit down for a formal meditation, you are internalizing your attention from the body and mind and resting your awareness on the Self, or your concept of God. When you are asleep, you can do the same. The difference is that instead of internalizing your attention from thoughts, you are internalizing your attention from the dreams. You can choose to rest your awareness on Self or divinity, while your dreams may or may not continue to play out in the background of your consciousness. You can continue your contemplations throughout the night. Hold in your awareness of that which you want to know as your body falls asleep, and maintain that focus into superconscious sleep. Then you can have the answers to your spiritual questions revealed to you, when you otherwise would be lost in unconsciousness.

The basic procedure for yogic sleep follows.

Yogic Sleep Process

Step 1: Meditate for 20 minutes to clear your mind and calm your nervous system. Practicing alternate nostril breathing, followed by chanting through the chakras, are ideal techniques for this purpose.

Step 2: Lie down on your back. Use pillows to support your head as needed. Place a pillow under your knees to support your lower back.

Step 3: Give your attention to your feet. Breathe in a relaxed even manner. As you breathe, imagine you can feel the breath flowing into your feet on the inhale, and flowing out on the exhale. Be aware of how your feet feel without judgment. Simply observe the sensations you notice in your feet as you breathe. Focus on the feet for three to five complete breaths.

Step 4: Move your attention to your ankles and lower legs. Repeat Step 3, while being aware of your ankles and lower legs.

Step 5: Taking your time, allowing your body to relax with each exhale. Repeat the same process in Step 3 at:

- the knees and upper legs
- the pelvis and buttocks region of your body
- the belly and lower back
- the chest and upper back
- the shoulders and down to the arms and hands

- the neck
- at the face and head

Focus on each area fully as you shift your awareness to each section of the body.

Step 6: Once you have brought your awareness throughout your entire body, breathing as you go, then turn your attention to the entire body. Feel the body as a whole, not in parts, but as one seamless beautiful unity. Feel the warmth of your core. Bring your awareness to the organs within the torso, the spine and brain. Continue to breathe in a relaxed, even manner. Feel as though the breath is not just entering and leaving through your nostrils, but through your body as a whole. Feel as though your whole body is inhaling and exhaling the life breath. Do this for five breaths.

Step 7: Now move your attention fully into your spine. Consolidate your attention on the first chakra, and mentally chant "Lum." Feel that the syllable "Lum" is pulsing through the root chakra with each repetition. Hold your attention at the first chakra in this way for three breaths. (Remember, the "u" in each of these seed syllables is pronounced as in the English word "run".)

Step 8: Next, move your attention to the second chakra, and mentally chant "Vum." Feel that the syllable "Vum" is pulsing through the second chakra with each repetition. Hold your attention at this chakra in this way for three breaths.

Step 9: Next, move your attention to the third chakra, and mentally chant "Rum." Feel that the syllable "Rum" is pulsing through the third chakra with each repetition. Hold your attention at this chakra in this way for three breaths.

Step 10: Next, move your attention to the fourth chakra, and mentally chant "Yum." Feel that the syllable "Yum" is pulsing through the fourth chakra with each repetition. Hold your attention at this chakra in this way for three breaths.

Step 11: Next, move your attention to the fifth chakra, and mentally chant "Hum." Feel that the syllable "Hum" is pulsing through the fifth chakra with each repetition. Hold your attention at this chakra in this way for three breaths.

Step 12: Next, move your attention to the sixth chakra, and mentally chant "Om." Feel that the syllable "Om" is pulsing through the sixth chakra with each repetition. Hold your attention at this chakra in this way for three breaths.

Step 13: Next, move your attention to the seventh chakra, and mentally chant "Bum." Feel that the syllable "Bum" is pulsing through the seventh chakra with each repetition. Hold your attention at this chakra in this way for six breaths.

Step 14: Now repeat Steps 10, 11 and 12, yet reversing the order. During the last step you were focused on the crown chakra. Repeat the process back down from the seventh chakra to the sixth chakra, to the fifth chakra, and concluding at the fourth chakra. Use the same breathing and seed syllable chanting procedures appropriate to each chakra as described previously.

Step 15: After focusing on the fourth chakra for three breathing cycles, stop chanting "Yum." Begin chanting "Om" at the fourth chakra. At the same time hold your awareness at the sixth chakra. Now you are holding your attention at both the fourth and sixth chakra, while chanting "Om." Feel as though the syllable "Om" is pulsing gently at both the fourth and sixth chakra simultaneously.

Step 16: Continue maintaining your awareness at the fourth and sixth chakra while chanting "Om." Let your body relax. It will eventually fall asleep. Use your gentle will power to maintain your attention at the fourth and sixth chakra to keep your consciousness awake and aware. These chakras are the anchors for your consciousness.

With the practice of this technique, you will begin to experience a state of alert-yet-relaxed awareness, as your body falls asleep and you begin to dream. It will be as though you are watching the sleep process occur as an observer.

This is not an easy skill to master and often takes many months of practice to begin to get the feel for it. The better your daily meditation practice, and the greater ease you have experiencing superconsciousness in your regular upright meditation sessions, the easier will be yogic sleep. This is because the same subtle awareness is required for success. If you are able to remain as the observer and hold your attention on your chosen point of focus in meditation, you will use the same subtle observational skills as your body falls asleep.

The time will come when you will easily recognize that your body is asleep, yet you are still conscious. Your perceptions will be the same as they are when your attention is fully internalized in meditation. What is this like? You are aware of the fact you exist. You are aware of the rise and fall of thoughts and images in your mind. You may also be aware of your passing emotions. Memories may come to your attention, yet you remain as the witnessing observer. You are more than likely not aware of your body. You are probably not aware of the environment around you either. It is as if you have become fully that little voice in your head that perceives and comments on everything.

At this stage, you can begin to strengthen your capacity to continue your meditation and contemplative practices while your body is asleep. This will require your will power and imagination.

Will power is required because just like your mind will wander into daydreams while your body is perfectly awake and active in the world, the same will happen while you are internally awake as the body sleeps. For example, you can be driving down the road or cooking a meal and your body can continue its activity, yet you may be lost in the thoughts of events from many hours to many years ago.

It is easier to recognize when this happens when you are awake, because you will have the body as an anchor to remind you of the task you are doing. Daydream too long and the car will veer or the chopping knife will slip from your hands. When you do not have the body or external environment as an anchor, if you lose your focus as you attempt to practice yogic sleep, all is lost. More than likely you will be sucked into the unconscious world of dreams without a chance to try again until you wake up and start over.

Learning to master your will to stay focused is a necessity as you practice yogic sleep. The closest experience I can compare it to is trying to force yourself to stay awake when you are extremely tired and all your eyelids want to do is close. That is what mastering your will in this kind of process feels like. However, it is different than that because when you are tired, really the only thing that will ultimately revive you is to sleep. Keeping yourself alert and focused as your body sleeps only requires you overcome the habit of drifting into unconsciousness when the body sleeps, which is common to everyone. Sleeping when the body is tired is natural. Becoming unconscious when the body sleeps is a habit. As time passes, you will realize this. You only have to overcome that natural tendency to lose awareness and drift into the unconscious during sleep.

After you can hold your focus internally during sleep, next you engage your imagination. You can either call into your awareness a thread of contemplation and focus intensely on that until realization dawns. This is often very profound. Or you can use your imagination to feel as though you are sitting in your typical meditation posture and practicing your usual meditation protocols. Both of these approaches will have the same effect. They will further clarify your awareness and allow you to continue your meditation practices throughout the night, with no one being the wiser.

An entire volume on yogic sleep is required to explore all the subtle complexities of the process. More than likely it will take you some time to master what I have described and intimated in the last dozen pages. Once you have these processes mastered you can deepen your studies into the uses of yogic sleep by exploring Carl Jung's ideas on active imagination or other texts like Tenzin Wangyal Rinpoche's book on Tibetan Dream Yoga. Yet the proper foundation to make the most of these other avenues has been laid out in this chapter. To conclude, let's discuss a few final points on the matter of yogic sleep.

There are some aids to be aware of to assist the process of yogic sleep. Diet and daily activity has a noticeable impact on one's capacity to practice yogic sleep. Eating heavy foods, hard-to-digest foods or overly processed foods can tax the body and make one require more and deeper sleep. The regular use of stimulants and recreational drugs can have the same effect. Some people find eating garlic, onions, meat and oily fried foods makes it harder to practice. A diet of fresh vegetables and fruits tend to make it easier.

If you attempt to practice yogic sleep, you want to be aware of the effect of the foods you eat. Experience will teach you which ones make you more inert and dull and which ones allow you to sleep more lightly and pleasantly. A light pleasant sleep is the easiest kind for which to try and practice yogic sleep.

Days that are filled with endless activity, ceaseless stimulation and tiring company can make yogic sleep harder to achieve. When we are exhausted from overwork or burnt out from social activity and entertainment, the body may more forcefully drive one into an unconscious sleep state. It is better to attempt this process when you are well-rested and have had a balanced day of rest and activity.

Yogic sleep can be practiced sleeping in any posture, but I have found that sleeping on one's back gives the best results. If you cannot sleep on your back, consider working with a healthcare provider to make it possible. I was not able to sleep on my back for many years, but after working with massage therapists and chiropractors, it is my preferred method of sleeping. If you ultimately cannot sleep on your back, you can still practice. You may simply need to put more attention to the other aids mentioned.

Yogic sleep is not required to be practiced every night. It is perfectly fine to sleep like a normal human being when you want to. Do not attempt yogic sleep at the expense of not getting enough rest. Remember, at least in the beginning, the more tired you are, the less likely you will do it well. Yogic sleep begins to happen naturally as your internal clarity generated by the Kriya Yoga Vichara practice progresses. If you are like me and have always found dreams and dream work fascinating, you may be more inclined to regularly attempt yogic sleep. Again, only do this when you are healthy minded and well-rested. Try it one night, rest well the next few nights. Try it again and then rest the next.

When I first started actively attempting to practice yogic sleep, I spent many a night forcing myself into a light restless sleep. I was tired the next day and felt exhausted from what I perceived to be non-stop dreaming. In time, as I got the hang of it, I learned to truly let my body sleep as it is supposed to, while maintaining an alert presence. Do your best, but don't exhaust yourself trying. Eventually you will have direct experience of how this process works and a whole new world will be opened up for your spiritual practice.

Chapter Eleven

THE INTERNAL ALCHEMY OF KRIYA YOGA VICHARA

To completely realize the inner alchemy of Kriya Yoga Vichara requires an awareness of how karma is stored and activated within your astral body. This will allow you to more fully appreciate the value of the specific meditation and contemplative techniques outlined in this text.

Remember that every thought, memory, habit, tendency, belief, feeling, emotion or activity we experience is a karma. Karma is essentially an energetic pattern stored within our consciousness. Most karmas that define our limited sense of self (ego/personality) are stored along the spinal pathway and within the astral energy centers often referred to as chakras. By linking the life force in the spine to the breath through Kriya practices, we quicken the evolution of our individualized being by dissolving those stored energetic imprints. How is this done?

Each conscious repetition of Kriya pranayama has the effect of living one full year of healthy stress-free living. Healthy stress-free living naturally ripens our capacity for spiritual liberation. This is why most authentic spiritual traditions advise a lifestyle conducive to increasing one's health and minimizing stress. It helps to set the proper foundation for more intensive practices.

By practicing 14 Kriya Pranayamas twice a day for one year, the yogi effectively quickens his evolution by 10,220 years. If a yogi practices 24 Kriya Pranayamas twice a day for one year, the evolution is quickened by 17,520 years. Theoretically, practicing Kriya pranayama for a minimum of 24 times a day, twice a day, would achieve spontaneous spiritual liberation in approximately 57 years of human life. By this process, a million years of natural evolution is distilled into one lifetime.

By practicing Kriya pranayama we are using our will power to consciously direct our inner awareness to identify and resolve stored karmas before they have a chance to express experientially. By bringing conscious awareness to these karmas stored and imprinted within the chakra system, we can essentially burn out the karmas before they have a chance to express unconsciously in our day-to-day lives. This occurs through proper application of pranayama and chanting through the chakras.

By proper application of pranayama and chanting, I mean to circulate life force through the chakras, or to pay attention to the chakras while remaining alert and watchful. This is because for karmas to be "burnt," they need to be properly digested and integrated. Digestion and integration occurs through attention. This is why mechanical or hypnotic repetition of the techniques in this book will serve little spiritual value aside from general relaxation.

Our goal is complete liberation from karmic bondage. This will result in a state of freedom, knowledge, faith and ease within one's being. If there are seeds for discomfort, anxiety, fear or doubt within our energetic system, they will block or obscure the experience of spiritual freedom. When we meditate using potent transformational techniques, these seeds of discomfort are revealed to us. Then we may resolve them internally without having to experience a physical event or circumstance to fulfill their momentum.

Most people evolve through the slow process of living out their stored karmas. It goes like this. When a situation arises in your life, a sudden emotion overtakes you. You act compulsively or suffer from obsessive thinking. You are experiencing the results of unresolved karmas. If you are able to remain internally calm, alert and detached as the momentum of these inner karmic forces exhaust themselves, you are resolving a karma reflected in your objectified experience in the present moment.

Many people are not evolving at all. Because instead of remaining internally calm, alert and detached while karmas arise, they add fuel to the fire. They instead act out irrationally without stopping to consider the consequences of their thoughts or actions. More karma is then created, like an acoustic feedback loop.

When an electrical musical instrument experiences feedback, it is due to sound from the instrument, reflecting back to the instrument. This causes the instrument to vibrate even more. This builds up until it creates an ear-piercing squeal or howl. The only way to stop this feedback loop is to either unplug the instrument or turn it away from the sound waves that are creating the problem.

Our karma works the same way. At some time in the past, we may have begun a pattern of anger. In the present, an objective experience reflects to us an opportunity to face and integrate that pattern of anger. If we are able to watch the anger, accept it and let its energy pass, we are essentially unplugging from a potentially harmful feedback loop. If, on the other hand, we unconsciously engage the reflected anger in the present moment and in turn get even more angry, and act in such a way to cause more violence and aggression, we are allowing the feedback loop to grow stronger. It may become so strong that it then begins to define us and we become deaf to its influence.

It is at this point where the feedback loop has become a karma that can easily throw us into an unconscious state. This is the hardest kind of karma to deal with, because its vibration is so loud and so strong in our consciousness that we actually then define our Self through it. We would feel lost without it. When others bring it to our awareness, we take it as a personal attack, because it feels like they are attacking the very fabric of our being.

This is why spiritual practices that call us to remain as the observational witness who remains "present in the moment" are effective. Present moment awareness can end the feedback loop of karma.

These present-moment-awareness practices are still relatively slow in their capacity to provide an avenue for yogic liberation, because in our daily life we can only process one worldly experience at a time. Yet, this is perfectly acceptable and an excellent place to begin. Why? Because staying in present moment awareness during everyday experiences gives our inner consciousness strength to work through our subliminal karmas in deep meditation. Once we are strong enough in our meditation practice, we can rapidly work through unresolved karmas without having to experience their fruits in the objective world. We are then able to resolve karmas internally, cutting their potential objective expression off closer to the root.

At this point it must be said that I am in no way encouraging anyone to deny valid authentic emotional expression. In everyone's life there will be times to be angry, full of grief, fearful or any other emotion. Many well-meaning but repressed people might term these experiences as unhealthy or negative. They may even say that one does not have spiritual understanding if they see someone grieving over loss or angry at an injustice. You have an outward human role to play while your inner spiritual life matures. Being appropriate externally is just as important as being appropriate internally.

In my experience, if emotion is a natural expression of what is happening right now, it is valid and authentic. Emotions that are obsessively and compulsively entertained, when there is no actual reason, are the ones I see indicating a karmic seed. When a dear loved one dies, to be sad and overcome with tears is natural. It may take days, months or years to fully process that. That is natural. Yet to live one's life in fear of losing relationships because someone previously has left you, is no life at all. That is a life defined by past karma.

As your spiritual life ripens, you will be able to live as any normal human being would. All the joys and hardships of the world will be as much a part of your life as anyone else's life. Yet internally you will remain clear and peaceful. Even in the midst of anger or grief, you will be internally centered. You will know the emotions are passing waves on the ocean of consciousness. You will express them outwardly, but internally you will know they do not define your infinite being. You will be free while living, and if you do it right, no one will ever know the difference. Now let's return to our inner work of resolving karmas before they have a chance to express.

What is the experience of resolving karmas internally? First we must know how to recognize our karma internally. Karmas can present themselves as images within the mind. They can arise as near or distant memories. Emotions or feelings within the body can indicate the presence of unintegrated karma. Repetitive or compulsive thoughts are also a sign of subliminal karmas, with the potential to express in our future objective experience.

This is why beginning meditators may feel they cannot meditate, because their first attempts reveal to their mind all the random thoughts and emotions that have not been properly digested. In actuality, they are doing exactly what needs to be done. By engaging a simple meditation technique they are then becoming aware of all the unresolved karmas on the surface of their consciousness. This is the first step of meditation, yet beginners interpret it to mean they are failing because they have the expectation that meditation should result in a perfectly tranquil state. That tranquility cannot arise until the surface debris of mental clutter and confusion has been acknowledged and integrated.

When we practice Kriya techniques that circulate our life force through the microcosmic astral solar system of the spine, we may internally activate a stored karma. Remaining awake, alert yet relaxed and watchful throughout this process, karmas will reveal themselves within our consciousness. As they flash through our awareness, they are being resolved or "burnt." Again, even intermediate or advanced meditators may become frustrated with this process.

An advanced meditator may have been meditating for years, yet still experiences internal distractions preventing her from accessing a profound state of yogic Samadhi. This is because rather than integrating the arising distraction through validating it and honoring its energy, she pushes it away aggressively, not wanting to face whatever that distraction may be. Because if she were meditating well, she would not have any distractions, right? Wrong.

Yet again we see the error. Meditation practices do not cause us to experience peace and tranquility. They reveal to us what is blocking that peace and tranquility which IS our natural state. Meditation practices cannot force us into tranquility or Self-realization. Meditation practices are tools, which reveal the unresolved karmic layers that block our direct experience and perception of the peace and being that is WHAT we are beyond all concepts and notions.

This is why Vichara contemplation on the question, "Who am I?", is so important within the process. As we practice Vichara, we are more easily aware of our true nature. When we are aware of our true nature, we do not overly identify with the problematic energy patterns of our karma and are able to resolve karma with objectivity and detachment. Remember the opening quote from the sage Vasistha at the beginning of this text.

"Verily, birds are able to fly with their two wings: even so both work and knowledge together lead to the supreme goal of liberation. Not indeed work alone nor indeed knowledge alone can lead to liberation: but, both of them together form the means to liberation."

Live from the knowledge that you are not ultimately defined by the transient karmas that seem so real and define you as limited human being. Work your karma out by remaining present in everyday interactions and clearing out your subliminal karmas through techniques in deep meditation. Then rest in the aftereffects of tranquility-Self-realization, which is your natural immortal state. It becomes easier the more you do it. Eventually it requires very little effort. But the hard work must be done first.

It may take a while before you catch a glimpse of the tranquility of Self-realization. That does not mean you are failing, it simply means you have more work to do before you get to the bottom of the karmic pile to see the Self-shining light beneath it. Do not ask, "How long is it going to take?" It will take as long as it takes. Don't give up because you don't know how long its going to take. You are going to have to do it one day! The longer you wait, the more effort it will take when you finally decide to address the issue. Do not be taken in by anyone who tells you it will happen spontaneously without any self-effort on your part or that any guru-savior can do it for you.

Another subtle point to remember is that while we want to resolve and integrate our karmas, we don't want to be incessantly looking for more karma. Our directive is to resolve what is presented. If nothing is presented then we rest in our nature of pure awareness. Many people interested in meditation or psychological transformation are not happy unless they have some trauma to discover and work through or some deep secret to reveal. This is not the work we are doing. **Pure awareness has to be enough for you.** Otherwise, you will continue experiencing karma.

Consciousness is both infinite and eternal. The abstract-intelligence-pure-conscious aspect of reality is infinite and eternal. The temporal-maya-perceptual-experience aspect is also infinite and eternal. These are what most people term Spirit and Nature. Ultimately, they are the same thing. (You can contemplate that on your own, but for now, try to take my word for it.) This is important to remember, because if you go looking for more karma to be revealed, you will always find it. There is no shortage of it. It is part of Nature, which is eternal and infinite, too. If you focus on fully immersing your Self in Spirit, or the pure conscious aspect of eternal infinite life, you will be able to readily see the relationship between Spirit and Nature. Then you will no longer get confused and define yourself only as limited egotistical being drowning in an ocean of karma.

The alchemical steps required for this path to work can be summarized below:

Step 1 – Learn to master your attention. Through training your mind to stay in one place through meditation, you increase your capacity for focus and attention. Your attention may be scattered by your choices of entertainment, lack of rest, and dramatic relationships. Your mind may have difficulty focusing because of the foods you eat or other substances you ingest. Your body may not be strong enough or disciplined enough to stay upright, relaxed, yet fully present, to focus on any activity for long. The first four limbs of yoga as described by Patanjali give a complete description of what works best as a foundation to master one's attention.

You must attend to your life, and arrange it in such a way, that you have the greatest likelihood of success in mastering your attention focus. Essentially it comes down to this. Eat well. Choose your companions wisely. Exercise for a strong and healthy body. Get enough rest. Don't overstimulate yourself. Do your best to be as kind as possible. Train yourself in meditation daily.

Step 2 – Direct your attention inward. Once you can focus and your attention has been mastered, now you find a suitable object of contemplation on which to focus. The Kriya meditation techniques described in this book provide excellent tools for inner focus.

Gain proficiency in the techniques. Become comfortable sitting quietly with your attention fully interiorized from any external experience. In time, you will even see thoughts and emotions as an external experience from your very Self. The limb of Yoga called Pratyahara is what you are now developing.

Step 3 – Contemplate that which you want to know. Once you can focus and hold your attention within, now you are ready to directly commune with your Self, the source of all knowledge and realization.

The practice of Vichara is now your focus. By exploring the threads of contemplation intensively with an interiorized awareness, you are prepared for Self-revealed knowledge. Now you can learn directly, "what you are," "what God is" or "what does it really mean to be enlightened."

The processes described by Patanjali called Dharana and Dhyana now become active. Dharana is resting your awareness, internally, without distraction on that which you want to know. Dhyana is absorbing your attention, to the exclusion of all else, into that point of inward focus.

Step 4 – Patiently wait for the inner realization to be revealed to you. As you keep your attention inwardly focused, you will become aware of all the karmas that prevent you from directly realizing your chosen theme of contemplation. So long as you stay attentive and true to the process, all those karmas will fall away. In time, when there are no other karmas to obscure your perception of truth, that which you are contemplating will dawn in your awareness in a flash, as if you knew it all along. Then you experience what Patanjali calls Samadhi, or perfect cognitive absorption.

It is during Step 4 that you will be rapidly digesting and integrating your karmic load. Think of it like this. If you want to be Self-realized, you have to release all the thoughts, notions and concepts that you cling to that prove to your experience that you are not Self-realized. When you sit down and focus on being Self-realized, everything that arises as a distraction in your consciousness, while you are attempting the process, is a revelation of what has been blocking your direct perception. This awareness gives you the ability to look beyond the distractions to rest in your pure conscious nature, the Eternal I, the Self.

Your task is to stay focused, and let all those concepts and notions exhaust themselves. When there are no more reasons arising in your consciousness contrary to Self-realization, it will be experienced spontaneously.

This is the work of Kriya Yoga Vichara. At its conclusion, you will know what you are beyond name and form. You will be able to function in the world effortlessly, seeing all the sorrows and joys as an expression of the one undivided consciousness, which is your very Self. All your concepts and philosophies about why life happens the way it does, or what God is, will vanish. You will have direct access to immediate knowing of the truth in all matters, and if you don't, you won't mind. You will trust your Self. Your faith will be real and final. There will be no more burning questions. You will live your life as you are meant to, without a doubt. You will then truly be...

Awake.

ABOUT THE AUTHOR

Ryan Kurczak was initiated into Kriya Yoga in 2000 and ordained to teach in 2005 by a direct student of Paramahansa Yogananda. Ryan is the author of many books on Spirituality and Astrology. Ryan works as an astrological consultant and teacher through Asheville Vedic Astrology.

For more information on Ryan's Kriya Yoga work, please visit the *LEARN KRIYA YOGA* section of:

www.AshevilleVedicAstrology.com

There you will find a downloadable 11-hour Kriya Yoga Training Course, a 26-hour Yoga Sutras Audio Course and a schedule for online live courses, when available.

Other Books By the Author

Kriya Yoga: Continuing the Lineage of Enlightenment

A Course in Tranquility

The Yogic Healing Siddhi Foundation Course
(Coming Soon)

Co-Authored with Richard Fish

The Art and Science of Vedic Astrology: The Foundation Course
(Vol. I)

The Art and Science of Vedic Astrology: Intermediate Principles of Astrology
(Vol. II)

Made in the USA
Middletown, DE
23 September 2022